VOLUME 1 CHAPTERS 1-16
WORKING PAPERS
TO ACCOMPANY

HILLMAN   KOCHANEK   NORGAARD

PRINCIPLES OF ACCOUNTING

SIXTH EDITION

INCLUDES OPERATING INSTRUCTIONS FOR THE PROBLEMS DISK AND
SPREADSHEET TEMPLATES DISKS, AND CHECKLIST OF KEY FIGURES

The Dryden Press
Harcourt Brace College Publishers
Fort Worth   Philadelphia   San Diego
New York   Orlando   Austin   San Antonio
Toronto   Montreal   London   Sydney   Tokyo

ISBN: 0-15-571220-9

Printed in the United States of America

TO THE STUDENT

Why Buy Working Papers?

The Working Papers to accompany *Principles of Accounting*, Sixth Edition, by Hillman, Kochanek, Norgaard, give you the maximum support for solving the assignment material at the end of each textbook chapter. The Working Papers let you concentrate on testing yourself on the principles and the procedures of accounting rather than taking time to hunt for generic forms pads or make up your own. Each working paper is a perfect fit with its matching test item—customized by the same authors who created the text assignments, even named and numbered the same.

This book of Working Papers will make you more productive in four major ways:

1. It contains the **exact forms required** on which the instructor will ask you to answer and solve each Exercise, A and B Problem, Practice Case, Business Decision and Communication Problem, and Ethical Dilemma at the end of every textbook chapter, as well as the required forms for the Mini Practice Sets after Chapters 4 and 12.

2. It contains **operating instructions for the Spreadsheet Templates Disks**. They allow you to solve selected labeled problems in the textbook using customized computer forms called **templates** using Lotus 1-2-3 spreadsheet software.

3. It contains **basic operating instructions for using the Problems Disk**, general and special ledger software that works with selected labeled textbook problems. This software performs like the accounting software you'll use in practice.

4. It contains a **Checklist of Key Figures**. This allows you to check your work for accuracy against the authors' own figures before turning in an assignment to the instructor.

How to Use the Working Papers

To use the Working Papers, simply turn to the assigned exercise, problem, or case in the textbook, page to the corresponding test item form in the Working Papers, and begin the assignment with the required forms before you. The Working Papers are listed by chapter and by assignment number. They match the assignment number and title in the textbook.

The Working Papers contain the form to match each answer required, whatever its type:

- Lined forms for written answers.

- Columnar forms, with the correct number of columns needed for tabular answers.

- Forms for each type of ledger, journal, special journal, and financial statement.

- Unique forms that frame answers in the special format supplied in the textbook.

As a learning aid, the Working Papers provide table, journal, ledger, and statement heads for the first two chapters but generally discontinue their use in later chapters. The number of blank lines should be adequate room for filling in the answer.

For most assignments, a single set of Working Papers is usually common to both A and B Problems; your instructor will assign either one or the other. Occasionally the A problem is different from the B problem; in such cases, Working Papers are supplied for both A and B.

Forms that are too large to fit on a single page have been moved into a foldout section at the back of the book. When working an assignment, **check for the cross-reference to foldouts** that appears below the number and title of that assignment in the Working Papers.

Be sure to write your name and section number on each page in the space provided before you tear out and turn in an assignment; space has been left for this at the top of every form.

CONTENTS

To the Student   iii
Operating Instructions for Problems Disk   P-1
     The Software Program   P-1
     Textbook Problems   P-1
     Getting Started   P-2
Operating Instructions for Spreadsheet Templates Disks I and II   S-1
     Introduction   S-1
     Textbook Problems and Template File Names   S-1
     Booting the Hillman Template Disk   S-3
     Retrieving a File   S-3
     Entering Labels   S-3
     Entering the Problem Number   S-3
     Entering Amounts   S-3
     Entering Formulas   S-3
     Printing the Work Sheet   S-4
     Saving Your Results in a File   S-4
     Quitting the Spreadsheet Software   S-4
Checklist of Key Figures for Exercises and Problem   CL-1–CL-31
Working Papers

Chapter	1	An Accounting Information System	1-1–1-31
Chapter	2	Processing Business Transactions	2-1–2-51
Chapter	3	Adjusting Entries	3-1–3-45
Chapter	4	Completion of the Accounting Cycle	4-1–4-63
		Mini Practice Set I	4-65–4-86
Chapter	5	Accounting for a Merchandising Business	5-1–5-51
Chapter	6	Special Journals and Accounting Systems	6-1–6-66
Chapter	7	Payroll System	7-1–7-29
Chapter	8	Internal Control and Cash	8-1–8-39
Chapter	9	Accounts Receivable and Bad Debts Expense	9-1–9-47
Chapter	10	Short-term Financing	10-1–10-51
Chapter	11	Inventories and Cost of Goods Sold	11-1–11-49
Chapter	12	Long-term Assets	12-1–12-37
		Mini Practice Set II	12-39–12-51
Chapter	13	Financial Reporting Issues	13-1–13-39
Chapter	14	Partnership Accounting	14-1–14-41
Chapter	15	Corporations: Paid-in Capital	15-1–15-51
Chapter	16	Additional Stockholders' Equity Transactions and Income Disclosures	16-1–16-47

Operating Instructions
for Problems Disk
by Leon Hanoville

Following are brief instructions on how to use the Hillman Problems Disk to solve selected problems in Chapters 1–28 of *Principles of Accounting*, Sixth Edition, by Hillman, Kochanek, and Norgaard. More complete instructions are available on the Problems Disk program, which is summarized below.

The Software Program

The Problems Disk is a stand-alone, compiled software program that allows you to complete selected financial accounting problems. Depending on the problem at hand, you will be able to journalize entries in general journals and some special journals, post entries to general ledgers and some special ledgers, and even complete financial statements.

The program is specific to selected problems from your textbook. You can only use the Problems Disk for these selections. The program is not flexible enough to allow you to work on other problems. (If you are interested in using an open-ended accounting system, one that allows posting to general journals and greater flexibility in accessing and printing information, you may wish to ask your bookstore for *The Real-Time Advantage: An Introduction to Computerized Accounting* by Yasuda and Wanlass.)

Textbook Problems

To identify which problems can be solved using the Problems Disk, look for the special disk logo next to the problem numbers in your textbook. The problems are also identified by chapter and problem number in the Main Menu of the Problems Disk and in the following list.

Problem Numbers

P2–30A & B
P2–32A & B
P3–28A & B
P4–31A & B
P5–31A & B
P6–32A & B
P6–33A & B
P9–31A & B
P10–27A & B
P10–29A & B
P12–35A & B
Ch. 12 Practice Case
P15–29A & B
Ch. 15 Practice Case
P16–29A & B
P16–30A & B
P17–28A & B

Getting Started

Your instructor may choose to supply you with instructions modified to match the computer system currently in use on your campus. Otherwise, use the following instructions.

Starting from a Floppy Disk

These instructions assume you are using an IBM PC or compatible DOS-based computer with one or more floppy drives, and that you will be booting with DOS version 2.1 or higher. It is further assumed that you know how to boot the machine with DOS. (Note that if you have only one floppy drive, the computer may periodically ask you to insert the Data Disk in that drive.)

1. Obtain the DOS A prompt as shown:

   A>

2. Remove the DOS disk before proceeding.

3. Insert the Problems Disk in Drive A and close the drive door.

4. Type **PROBDISK** at the prompt and press the **ENTER** or **<RETURN>** key, as shown:

   A>PROBDISK <ENTER>

5. Follow further instructions onscreen. After displaying one or two preliminary screens, the computer will display the Main Menu.

6. The Main Menu will allow you to highlight your next choice, which could include specific problems. Note the HELP option available from the Main Menu. Use this option to learn more about the operation of the program.

Starting from a Hard Disk Drive

These instructions assume that the Problems Disk program has already been installed in a directory or subdirectory of a hard disk drive on an IBM PC-XT, -AT, PS 2, or compatible DOS-based computer. (For instructions on how to install the program, use the DOS command **TYPE HDREAD** to display the HDREAD file on the distribution diskette.)

1. Obtain the DOS C prompt for the C directory or subdirectory of the hard disk drive, as shown:

   C:\HILLMAN>

2. Type **PROBDISK** at the prompt and press the **ENTER** or **<RETURN>** key, as shown:

   C:\HILLMAN>PROBDISK <ENTER>

3. Follow further instructions onscreen. After displaying one or two preliminary screens, the computer will display the Main Menu.

4. The Main Menu will allow you to highlight your next choice, which may include specific problems. Note the HELP option available on the Main Menu. Use this option to learn more about the operation of the program.

Operating Instructions
for Spreadsheet Templates Disks I and II
by Donald R. Davis

Disk I: Chapters 1–16
Disk II: Chapters 14–28

Introduction

Following are brief instructions on how to use the Hillman Template Disks to solve selected problems in Chapters 1–28 of *Principles of Accounting*, Sixth Edition, by Hillman, Kochanek, and Norgaard. More complete instructions on how to operate spreadsheet software can be found in the documentation furnished with Lotus 1-2-3. The following instructions also appear on the Hillman Template Disks.

You may move forward or backward through these instructions, if viewing them on a screen, by using the **PgUp** or **PgDn** keys. To print the instructions, hold the **ALT** key down and tap the **P** key. You may exit the instructions at any time by typing **/**, which will bring the command menu to the top of the screen.

Textbook Problems and Template File Names

The selected problems are designed to give you experience in seeing how a microcomputer and electronic spreadsheet software can be used to automate parts of the accounting process. Accounting packages supplied by software vendors may also be used to perform many of the same tasks, but they lack some of the flexibility provided by the electronic spreadsheet.

The selected problems in the text and their respective template file names are as follows:

Problem Numbers	Template Files
INSTRUCTIONS	AUTO123
P1–30A & B	P1–30
P2–31A & B	P2–31
P2–34A	P2–34
P3–27A & B	P3–27
P4–30A & B	P4–30
Ch. 4 Practice Case	P4–CASE
P5–32A & B	P5–32
P5–34A & B	P5–34
Ch. 6 Practice Case	P6–CASE
P7–24A & B	P7–24
P7–26A & B	P7–26
P8–30A & B	P8–30
P8–31A & B	P8–31
P9–32A & B	P9–32

Problem Numbers	Template Files
P10–25A & B	P10–25
P11–27A & B	P11–27
P11–30A & B	P11–30
P12–33A & B	P12–33
P13–36A & B	P13–36
P14–26A & B	P14–26
P14–31A & B	P14–31
P15–27A & B	P15–27
P16–31A & B	P16–31
P16–33A & B	P16–33
P17–29A & B	P17–29
P17–30A & B	P17–30
P18–31A & B	P18–31
P18–32A & B	P18–32
P19–32A & B	P19–32
P19–36A & B	P19–36
P20–29A & B	P20–29
P20–31A & B	P20–31
P20–33A & B	P20–33
P20–34A & B	P20–34
P21–27A & B	P21–27
P21–31A & B	P21–31
P22–29A & B	P22–29
P22–31A & B	P22–31
P23–27A & B	P23–27
P23–28A & B	P23–28
P24–33A & B	P24–33
P24–36A & B	P24–36
P25–27A & B	P25–27
P25–29A & B	P25–29
P25–30A & B	P25–30
P26–30A	P26–30
P26–31A & B	P26–31
P26–36A	P26–36

Problem Numbers	Template Files
P27–27A & B	P27–27
P27–31A & B	P27–31
P28–29A	P28–29
P28–30B	P28–30
P28–34A & B	P28–34

Booting the Hillman Template Disk (Your instructor may modify this procedure.)

1. Insert an IBM PC DOS disk (version 2.0 or higher) in Drive A and a Hillman Template Disk in Drive B, turn on the computer, and enter the date and time when prompted.

2. When the A> prompt appears, remove the DOS disk and insert a Lotus 1-2-3 system disk in Drive A. Type **123** and press the **ENTER** key. Answer the screen prompts and the Hillman Template Disk Instructions will be displayed.

Retrieving a File

Various series of keystrokes will be given to allow you to accomplish different tasks. Press each key slowly at first and observe the top of the screen to see how the menus are utilized.

To retrieve the template file for P1–30A, type **/FR**, use the **ARROW CURSOR** keys to highlight P1–30, and press the **ENTER** key. You may also enter the file name and press the **ENTER** key. The work sheet area will clear and be replaced by the template for the problem. A *template* is a work sheet that contains formulas but no data.

Entering Labels

Read the instructions for the problem on the screen, enter your name (which will appear on the second line of the screen), and press the **ENTER** key. Your name will now appear in the cell to the right of "NAME:" and on line 1 (the status line). You may press the **F2** key if you want to edit your name, or simply retype your name and press **ENTER** again. Use the **ARROW CURSOR** keys, the **BACKSPACE** key, and the **DEL** key for editing. You may also enter **/RE** and press the **ENTER** key to erase a cell.

If you attempt to type in a cell which is not supposed to be changed, the message "Protected Cell" will be displayed. Press the **ESC** key to continue.

Your name, a heading, or an account title are called *labels*. If a label is wider than the cell in which it is being typed, it will spill over into the next adjacent cell. A label is usually left justified within a cell and is indicated by an apostrophe (') to the left of the label in the status area at the top of the screen. You may center a label by entering a caret (^) to the left of the label or right justify a label by entering a quotation mark (").

Entering the Problem Number

Most of the template files are set up for the A version of the problem in the textbook. If you are working the B version, move the cursor using the arrow keys to the cell where P1–30A is located, press the **F2** key, press the **BACKSPACE** key (left arrow at top of keyboard), enter a **B**, and press the **ENTER** key. On some of the other problems you may also need to change A to B in the cell to the right of "VERSION:."

Entering Amounts

Move the cursor to the first "AMOUNT ?" cell where you will need to enter a number. Enter your number without a dollar sign or commas, but with a decimal point if needed. The cells have already been formatted

S–3

to insert dollar signs and commas where appropriate. Use the **PgUp**, **PgDn**, and cursor keys to search the rest of the template for cells requiring amounts or formulas, and to view the results.

Entering Formulas

In some of the problems you will notice cells containing the word "FORMULA?." This means you will have to determine the formula for this cell. Following are examples of valid formulas:

+B5+B6	(+ = addition. Adds the amounts in cells B5 and B6. The + sign to the left of B5 is required to prevent B5 being printed as a label rather than the value of cell B5.)
+B5–B6	(– = subtraction)
1.1*C5	(* = multiplication)
+D5/D4	(/ = division)
+E6^	(^ = exponentiation: +E6^2 = E6 squared.)
(B1+B2)*A3	(The addition within the parentheses is computed before the multiplication takes place.)
((B1+B2)–C1)*D2	(The expression within the innermost parentheses is added first, next the subtraction, and finally the multiplication.)
@SUM(A1..A5)	(Another way of adding the amounts in cells A1 through A5.)

See your spreadsheet software documentation for additional examples of formulas.

Printing the Work Sheet

To print the work sheet, hold the **ALT** key down and tap the **P** key. Pressing the **P** key too long will result in multiple copies. **A wide carriage printer or one capable of compressed type is required for some work sheets.** The print string used for compressed type for your printer may need to be entered under the Print Options Setup Menu (Enter **/PPOS**). See your spreadsheet software documentation for additional information on printing.

Saving Your Results in a File

Enter **/FS** and enter a new file name such as P1–30A if you are doing the A version of the problem. **Do not use P1–30 as the name, as this will destroy the original blank template file.** After entering the new file name, press **ENTER** and your work sheet will be saved to your disk. If you have saved it before, the words CANCEL and REPLACE will appear in the status area at the top of the screen. Press **R** to replace the previous file with your new one, or **C** to cancel the command. If you want to keep the previous version of the file, save your current work sheet under a different file name.

Quitting the Spreadsheet Software

Enter **/QY** and press the **ENTER** key. You may also have to enter **EY** to exit the system.

Harcourt Brace Jovanovich, Inc.; International Business Machines Corporation; Lotus Development Corporation, and the authors make no warranties, either express or implied, regarding the computer software, its merchantability, or fitness for any purpose.

Checklist of Key Figures for Exercises and Problems

Exercise or Problem	Req.	Check Figure
Chapter 1		
E1-17		No check figure.
E1-18		three
E1-19	1	$1,778.3
E1-20	5	$25,000
E1-21	a	-A, +L, or +OE
E1-22		+A, +L
E1-23		+A, -A
E1-24		Jun. 12, -A, +A
E1-25		Aug. 26, +A, +OE
E1-26	a	current liability
E1-27		Total assets, $199,000
E1-28		Total assets, $95,000
P1-29A		four
P1-30A		ConAgra, $4,278
P1-31A	1	$27,000
	2	$25,000
P1-32A	c	Total assets, $38,000
P1-33A	1	Cash, $17,450
	2	Total assets, $20,400
P1-34A		Capital, $27,500
P1-35A	4	$30,000
P1-29B		four
P1-30B		Southwestern Bell, $12,794
P1-31B	1	$17,000
	2	$13,000
	4	$5,000
P1-32B	c	Total assets, $55,000
P1-33B	1	Cash, $10,000
	2	Total assets, $16,700
P1-34B		Capital, $49,100
P1-35B	4	$100,000
PC	2	Capital, $38,100
	4	Total assets, $43,700
Chapter 2		
E2-16		10 accounts
E2-17	10	Increase
E2-18		Cash total credits, $3,200
E2-19		Cash bal., $8,000
E2-20		Mar. 5, dr. cash, $400
E2-21		Mar. 7, cr. Accounts Payable, $400

E2-22		Cash bal., $2,600
E2-23		$33,000
E2-24	a	Yes, $1,000, debit
E2-25	a	income statement
E2-26		$3,000
E2-27		Total assets, $36,000
P2-28A		21 accounts
P2-29A		Cash bal., $48,800
P2-30A	3	$43,000
P2-31A	1	$203,000
	4	Total assets, $190,000
P2-32A	3	$48,000
	4	Total assets, $44,000
P2-33A	1	capital, $23,900
	3	Total expenses, $25,100
P2-34A	1	Net income, $1,112.8
	3	5.26%
P2-28B		16 accounts
P2-29B		Cash bal., $29,100
P2-30B	3	$23,000
P2-31B	1	$129,000
	4	Total assets, $121,000
P2-32B	3	$57,400
	4	Total assets, $51,800
P2-33B	2	capital, $38,000
	3	Total property, plant, and equipment, $32,000
P2-34B	1	1989 expenses, $2,957.3
	2	1989, 4.26%
PC	5	$24,300
	6	Total assets, $22,700

Chapter 3

E3-12		$6,400
E3-13		$2,500
E3-14	a	$200
E3-15	1	$2,900
E3-16		Unearned, $45,500
E3-17	a	$300
E3-18		$18
E3-19	a	$1,200
E3-20	a	$800
E3-21	a	$9,000
E3-22	1	$6,000
E3-23	2	$90
E3-24	1	$2,800
P3-25A	a	$30
	c	$4,000

P3-26A	a	$300
	d	$4,800
P3-27A	c	$840
	g	$16,000
P3-28A	4	$170,040
	5	Total assets, $51,040
P3-29A	a	$1,600; Current asset, $200
P3-30A		Office Supplies dr., $1,400
P3-31A	1	Total assets, $101,380
P3-25B	a	$1,000
	c	$5,000
P3-26B	a	$500
	d	$2,700
P3-27B	c	$7,000
	g	$2,800
P3-28B	4	$133,480
	5	Total assets, $41,400
P3-29B	a	$700; expense, $36,400
P3-30B		Office Supplies dr., $600
P3-31B	1	Total assets, $92,380
PC	a	Office Supplies Expense dr., $3,500
	d	Professional Fees Revenue cr., $12,000

Chapter 4

E4-17		Net income, $15,000
E4-18		Net income, $17,500
E4-19		Net income, $1,000
E4-20		Net income, $8,900
E4-21	1	Interest Expense dr., $39
E4-22	1	Insurance Expense dr., $1,800
E4-23		Income Summary closing, $8,000
E4-24		Postclosing trial balance, $65,500
E4-25	2	Net Income, $20,400
E4-26		reverse four entries
E4-27		Income summary closing, $28,000
E4-28		Net income, $16,500; total stockholders' equity, $58,500
P4-29A	1	Net income, $12,600
	3	Total assets, $102,600
P4-30A	1	Net income, $28,000
P4-31A	4	Net income, $5,465
	8	$24,380
P4-32A	3	$49,000
P4-33A	1	$3,000
	2	$29,000
P4-34A		Income Summary bal., $389,900
P4-35A	2	Net income, $6,650
	3	Total assets, $227,700

P4-29B	1	Net income, $8,350
	3	Total assets, $56,100
P4-30B	1	Net income, $7,000
P4-31B	3	Net income, $850
	8	$19,590
P4-32B	3	$51,000
P4-33B	1	$15,600
	2	$60,450
P4-34B		Income Summary bal., $23,800 dr.
P4-35B	2	Net income, $14,750
	3	Total assets, $218,650
PC	1	Net income, $24,540
	2	Total assets, $40,800

Mini Practice Set I

Unadjusted trial balance, $23,700; net income, $(240); total assets, $18,900

Chapter 5

E5-16		Feb. 4, cr. Sales, $1,000
E5-17		Apr. 5, dr. Purchases, $2,000
E5-18		Sales, $7,200
E5-19		Sales discounts, $300
E5-20	1b	$30,000
E5-21		Gross margin, $8,900
E5-22		Net income, $4,000
E5-23	1	Adjusted trial bal. debit total, $37,000
E5-24		Kona net income, $7,000
		Hilo sales, $70,000
E5-25		Net income, $7,300
E5-26		Income summary closing, $7,300
E5-27	1	Purchases dr., $8,820
P5-28A		Feb. 18, Cash dr., $1,960; Feb. 28, Cash dr., $1,372
P5-29A		Gross margin on sales, $243,000
P5-30A	1	Net income, $13,000
P5-31A	2	Cash bal., $10,132
	3	Net income, $2,164
P5-32A	1	Net income, $32,000
	2	Total assets, $163,000
P5-33A	1b	Cost of goods sold, $1,460
	2b	Cost of goods sold, $1,449
P5-34A	1	1990, net operating margin, $545,939
	2	1990, net operating margin to net sales, 11.4%
P5-28B		Aug. 11, Cash cr., $9,405; Aug. 29, Cash dr., $1,764
P5-29B		Cost of goods sold, $572,000
P5-30B	1	Net loss, $(22,000)

P5-31B	2	Cash bal., $5,080
	3	Net income, $2,712
P5-32B	1	Net income, $69,100
	2	Total assets, $244,100
P5-33B	1b	Cost of goods sold, $2,490
	2b	Cost of goods sold, $2,483
P5-34B	1	1989, net operating margin, $1,482
	2	1989, net operating margin to net sales, 9.2%
PC	1	Net income, $9,000
	3	Total assets, $177,000

Chapter 6

E6-18		Apr. 2, cash receipts
E6-19		Sales journal total, $1,400
E6-20		Cash debit total, $17,628
E6-21		Purchases debit total, $10,200
E6-22		Cash credit total, $26,120
E6-23		Accounts Receivable bal., $50,000
E6-24		Accounts Receivable cr., $1,800
E6-25		Accounts Payable bal., $16,000
E6-26		Accounts Payable dr., $2,500
E6-27	a	Schedule of subsidiary ledger
E6-28	1	Cr.
E6-29	a	Cash receipts
	g	General journal
P6-30A	1	Sales total, $10,200
	3	Accounts Receivable bal., $2,000
P6-31A	1	Purchases journal, Accounts Payable, $10,900
	3	Accounts Payable bal., $2,500
P6-32A	3	Cash bal., $4,432
	4	$11,145
P6-33A	1	Cash receipts, cash total, $115,610
		Cash payments, cash total, $59,055
P6-34A		Cash payments, $30,800
P6-35A	1	Accounts Receivable bal., $2,160
P6-36A		Cash payments, cash total $75,000
P6-30B	1	Sales total, $8,400
	3	Accounts Receivable bal., $2,000
P6-31B	1	Purchases journal, Accounts Payable, $10,500
	3	Accounts Payable bal., $4,000
P6-32B	3	Cash bal., $5,327
	4	$16,547
P6-33B	1	Cash receipts, cash total, $66,141; Cash payments, cash total, $29,572
P6-34B		Cash payments, $101,000
P6-35B	1	Accounts Payable bal., $3,470
P6-36B		Cash payments, cash total $50,800

| PC | 3 | Cash bal., $11,318; Accounts Receivable bal., $900; Accounts Payable bal., $1,300 |
| | 5 | Net income, $935; total assets, $13,318 |

Chapter 7

E7-12		$624
E7-13		Dave Eber, $69
E7-14		Dave Eber, $51.38
E7-15	a	$161.56
E7-16		$133.55
E7-17	a	Salaries and Wages Payable cr., $5,475
E7-18		$61,150
E7-19		$131.25
E7-20		State unemployment, $40
E7-21		$62,559
E7-22	a	Vacation Pay Expense dr., $1,920
E7-23		No check figure.
P7-24A		Net pay, $1,380.45
P7-25A	1	Salaries and Wages Payable cr., $6,430
P7-26A	1	Net pay, $2,916.78
P7-27A		Net pay, $1,716.12
P7-28A	1	Salaries and Wages Payable cr., $3,030.50
P7-29A	1	Vacation Pay Expense dr., $16,000
P7-30A		No check figure.
P7-24B		Net pay, $1,280.30
P7-25B	1	Salaries and Wages Payable cr., $5,680
P7-26B	1	Net pay, $2,404.95
P7-27B		Net pay, $1,693.00
P7-28B	1	Salaries and Wages Payable cr., $4,123.50
P7-29B	1	Vacation Pay Expense dr., $35,000
P7-30B		No check figure.
PC	1	Net pay, $2,529.04
	4	Payroll Tax Expense dr., $139.36

Chapter 8

E8-16	2	Cash cr., $602
E8-17		Cash shortage, $4
E8-18	1	d
	6	c
E8-19		Adjusted bal., $2,800
E8-20		Net cash dr., $29.79
E8-21		Adjusted cash bal., $5,400
E8-22		Adjusted cash bal., $7,100
E8-23		Vouchers Payable total, $8,625
E8-24		Vouchers Payable total, $6,150
E8-25		Vouchers Payable total cr., $14,000
E8-26		Vouchers Payable cr., $2,500

P8-27A		Shortage of $860
P8-28A	2	Cash cr., $350
	3	Cash cr., $408
P8-29A	1	Adjusted cash bal., $4,250
P8-30A	1	Adjusted cash bal., $4,700
P8-31A	1	Adjusted cash bal., $1,290
P8-32A	1	Voucher register, Vouchers Payable total, $11,375; check register, Vouchers Payable total, $4,775
	2	Vouchers Payable bal., $4,200
P8-33A	1b	Cash dr., $2,564.10
P8-27B		No check figure.
P8-28B	2	Cash cr., $595
	3	Cash cr., $412
P8-29B	1	Adjusted cash bal., $3,400
P8-30B	1	Adjusted cash bal., $8,300
P8-31B	1	Adjusted cash bal., $5,380
P8-32B	1	Voucher register, Vouchers Payable total, $23,140; check register, Vouchers Payable total, $12,940
	2	Vouchers Payable bal., $6,200
P8-33B	1	Cash removed, $2,220
PC	1	Adjusted cash bal., $42,974
	2	Adjusted cash bal., $62,773

Chapter 9

E9-16	1	Net accounts receivable, $59,000
E9-17		Dec. 31, Bad Debts Expense dr., $6,000
E9-18	a	Bad Debts Expense dr., $7,700
E9-19	a	Bad Debts Expense dr., $5,300
E9-20	2	Accounts Receivable, net realizable value, $94,000
E9-21	3	Allowance for Doubtful Accounts cr., $2,978
E9-22		Apr. 18, Accounts Receivable cr., $930
E9-23	2d	Net accounts receivable, $60,160
E9-24		Cash dr., $28,800
E9-25		Total, current assets, $64,800
E9-26		No check figure.
E9-27	c	Net realizable value, $0
E9-28		Cash received from customers, $577,700
P9-29A		Jun. 10, 1994, Allowance for Doubtful Accounts cr., $500; Dec. 2, 1994, Allowance for Doubtful Accounts dr., $120
P9-30A	1	Dec. 31, 1994, Bad Debts Expense dr., $4,900
	2	Dec 31, 1994, Allowance for Doubtful Accounts bal., $15,000 cr.
P9-31A	2	Dec. 8, Accounts Receivable bal., $27,600 dr.
P9-32A	2	Total uncollectible accounts, $3,942
	3	Bad Debts Expense dr., $3,542
P9-33A	2	Net income, $64,500
	3	Accounts receivable, $70,000
P9-34A	2a	Bad Debts Expense, $1,800
	2b	Bad Debts Expense, $2,160

P9-35A	1	Bad Debts Expense dr., $26,957,000
P9-29B		Mar. 4, 1994, Allowance for Doubtful Accounts cr., $800; Dec. 1, 1994, Allowance for Doubtful Accounts dr., $1,270
P9-30B	1	Dec. 31, 1994, Bad Debts Expense dr., $2,900
	2	Dec. 31, 1994, Allowance for Doubtful Accounts bal., $9,000 cr.
P9-31B	2	Nov. 8, Accounts Receivable bal., $12,410 dr.
P9-32B	2	Total uncollectible accounts, $6,075
	3	Bad Debts Expense dr., $6,125
P9-33B	2	Net income, $108,400
	3	Net accounts receivable, $137,800
P9-34B	2a	Bad Debts Expense, $6,700
	2b	Bad Debts Expense, $7,450
P9-35B	5	Accounts Receivable, $253,973,000
PC	1h	Allowance for Doubtful Accounts cr., $10,086
	2	Total current assets, $1,047,614

Chapter 10

E10-12		Jul. 14, 1993, note maturity date is Jan. 10, 1994
E10-13		Aug. 24, 1993, note maturity value $4,045
E10-14	a	APR equals 15%
E10-15		Jun. 13, 1993, Cash cr., $6,360
E10-16		Total accrued interest, $491.95
E10-17		Dec. 16, 1993, Discount on Notes Payable dr., $180
E10-18		Dec. 31, 1993, Interest Payable cr., $150
E10-19		Oct. 19, 1993, Interest Revenue cr., $240
E10-20		Dec. 31, 1993, Interest Receivable dr., $234
E10-21		Dec. 5, 1993, Cash dr., $1,626.46
E10-22		Oct. 20, Cash dr., $5,464.66
E10-23		Books of Joe Link, Apr. 2, 1993, Interest Revenue cr., $7
E10-24	a	Made sale of $900 on account
P10-25A		Total accrued interest, $415.92
P10-26A	a	Annual effective interest = 48% per year
	b	Annual effective interest = 24% per year
P10-27A		Dec. 16, 1993, Discount on Notes Payable dr., $330
		Feb. 20, 1994, Cash cr., $6,150
P10-28A	2	The note given to the New York Bank is more favorable.
P10-29A		Dec. 28, 1993, Cash dr., $7,042.82; Jan. 12, 1994, Interest Receivable cr., $180
P10-30A		May 10, 1993, Interest Revenue cr., $26.40; Aug. 7, 1993, Cash dr., $3,308.76
P10-31A		Coca-Cola has 90% of its credit line unused
P10-25B		Total accrued interest, $377.25
P10-26B	a	Annual effective interest = 40% per year
	b	Annual effective interest = 20% per year
P10-27B		Apr. 17, 1993, Cash cr., $2,560; Dec. 16, 1993, Discount on Notes Payable dr., $120
P10-28B	2	The note given to the Village Bank is more favorable.

P10-29B		Dec. 12, 1993, Cash dr., $3,003.13; Jan. 16, 1994, Interest Receivable cr., $92.50
P10-30B		Jul. 30, 1993, Interest Revenue cr., $27; Aug. 24, 1993, Cash dr., $3,010.27
P10-31B		Montana Company should choose the Billings Bank loan.
PC		Aug. 19, 1993, Discount on Notes Payable dr., $650; Sep. 10, 1993, Cash dr., $24,011.48; Nov. 2, 1993, Notes Receivable Discounted dr., $24,000

Chapter 11

E11-13		Total cost, $29,550
E11-14	a	May 6, Purchases Returns and Allowances cr., $75
	b	May 8, Cost of Goods Sold dr., $540
E11-15		Gross margin on sales, $21,000
E11-16		Gross margin on sales, $18,000
E11-17	a	FIFO cost of goods sold, $500
	b	LIFO ending inventory, $550
E11-18		FIFO ending balance, 55 units; total cost, $17,875; LIFO ending bal., 55 units; total cost, $16,150
E11-19	b	Cost of Goods Sold, $943.80
E11-20		Ending bal., 500 units; total cost, $2,350
E11-21	a	FIFO net income, 1993, $60,000
	b	LIFO net income, 1994, $50,000
E11-22		Total cost, $23,760; total market, $22,900
E11-23		Estimated inventory, $73,400
E11-24		Ending inventory at cost, $117,000
E11-25		Gross margin, 1993, +$3,000; 1994, -$3,000
P11-26A	1	Cost of Goods Sold dr., $270,000
P11-27A	1	Weighted average cost of goods sold, $2,790
	3	LIFO ending inventory, $1,650
P11-28A	2	FIFO cost of goods sold, $2,825
	3	LIFO ending inventory, $900
P11-29A	1b	LIFO cost of goods sold, $124,000
	2	FIFO net income, $28,000
P11-30A	1	Estimated inventory, Sept. 30, 1993, $195,000
	2	Estimated ending inventory at cost, $38,500
P11-31A	1	Net income, 1994, $12,000
	2c	Dec. 31, 1993, owner's equity overstated by $4,000
P11-32A	1	Approx. 52%
	2	$2,116 million
P11-26B	1	Cost of Goods Sold dr., $405,000
P11-27B	1	Weighted average cost of goods sold, $3,500
	3	LIFO ending inventory, $1,650
P11-28B	2	FIFO cost of goods sold, $2,910
	3	LIFO ending inventory, $915
P11-29B	1b	LIFO cost of goods sold, $27,600
	2	FIFO net income, $3,600

P11-30B	1	Estimated inventory, Jan. 31, 1993, $96,000
	2	Estimated ending inventory at cost, $46,400
P11-31B	2	1994 net income overstated by $115,780
	3	Net decrease in owner's capital, $4,220
P11-32B	1	Approx. 58%
	2	$168,405,000
PC	1a	FIFO net income, $1,425
	2b	LIFO net income, $1,395

Chapter 12

E12-16		Total debits to Delivery Van account, $23,115
E12-17		Office Equipment dr., $4,508
E12-18		Cash cr., $3,224,000
E12-19	b	Depreciation Expense—Aircraft dr., $500,000
	d	Accumulated Depreciation—Aircraft cr., $93,500
E12-20	b	1993, $22,500
	c	1994, $51,480
E12-21	a	$1,800
E12-22	b	$4,240
E12-23	c	Revenue, Insurance Expense
	h	Capital, Accumulated Depreciation
	j	Capital, Goodwill
E12-24		1995: $32,000
E12-25		Dec. 31, 1995, Depreciation Expense—Freezer dr., $4,375
E12-26		Gain on Disposal of Plant Assets cr., $9,000
E12-27	2b	Loss on Disposal of Plant Assets dr., $1,500
	3a	Gain on Disposal of Plant Assets cr., $1,000
E12-28		Depletion cost for first year, $744,000
E12-29	c	N
	i	Depletion
	m	Depreciation
E12-30		Dec. 31, 1993, Franchise Amortization Expense dr., $10,500
E12-31		Dec. 31, 1994, Patent cr., $11,200
P12-32A	1	Total asset cost, $27,460
	2	Total expense, $1,500
P12-33A	1	Building, $125,000
	2	Depreciation Expense—Sorting Equipment dr., $70,000
P12-34A	3	Dec. 31, 1991, Depreciation Expense—Delivery Truck dr., $3,750
	4	Dec. 31, Depreciation Expense—Delivery Truck dr., $7,700
P12-35A		Dec. 31, 1993, Depreciation Expense—Carpet Cleaning System dr., $15,400; Jul. 3, 1995, Gain on Disposal of Plant Assets cr., $5,000
P12-36A	1	Automobile (new) dr., $88,875
	2	Loss on Disposal of Plant Assets dr., $4,875
P12-37A	1	Depletion cost in 1993, $2,820,000
	2	Cost of oil sold in 1993, $2,405,000
P12-38A	C1	Capital expenditure, tangible plant asset, $989,500
	C4	Capital expenditure, intangible asset, $372,000

Copyright © 1992 by Harcourt Brace Jovanovich, Inc. All rights reserved.

P12-32B	1	Total asset cost, $14,375
	2	Total expense, $917
P12-33B	1	Building, $32,000
	2	Depreciation Expense—Painting Equipment dr., $65,000
P12-34B	3	Dec. 31, 1991, Depreciation Expense—Dump Truck dr., $1,500
	4	Dec. 31, Depreciation Expense—Dump Truck dr., $5,700
P12-35B		Dec. 31, 1993, Depreciation Expense—Food Warming Equipment dr., $6,400; Jul. 31, 1995, Loss on Disposal of Plant Assets dr., $13,100
P12-36B	1	Drill Press (new) dr., $170,000
	2	Loss on Disposal of Plant Assets dr., $26,000
P12-37B	1	Depletion cost in 1993, $2,468,750
	2	Cost of oil sold in 1993, $2,775,000
P12-38B	C1	New addition, $908,800
	C4	Remaining asset balance on Dec. 31, 1993, $305,800
PC		Dec. 31, 1993, Depreciation Expense—Machinery dr., $3,540; Jan. 1, 1995, Accumulated Depreciation—Machinery dr., $6,300; Jul. 1, 1995, Cash cr., $22,880

Mini Practice Set II

	2	Net income, $155,207; total assets, $707,777
	5a1	Net income, $245,607
	5a3	Owner's equity, $435,507

Chapter 13

E13-21	a	materiality
	c	consistency
E13-22		Gross margin recognized, Feb., $24
E13-23		Gross margin for 1993, $1,095,000
E13-24		In average constant dollars, the increase in sales is $6,250
E13-25		Restated sales (1993 average constant dollars), 1992, $5,100,000
E13-26		Net income should really be a net loss of $(20,000)
E13-27		Value of land, $5,743
E13-28	1a	$31,250
	1b	$42,969
E13-29		Total, $2,905
P13-30A	c	Matching concept, conservatism
	e	Conservatism, historical cost, objectivity
P13-31A	b	Consistency, matching, full disclosure
	d	Revenue recognition, conservatism
P13-32A		Net income, $75,000; total assets, $270,000
P13-33A	1b	Large decrease in cost of goods sold
P13-34A	3	Monetary assets (i.e., Cash, Accounts receivable)
P13-35A		Net monetary liabilities Dec. 31, 1993, $(214,000); Purchasing power gain, $32,917
P13-36A	1	Purchasing power gain, $73,818
P13-30B	c	Entity concept
	e	Revenue realization, objectivity

P13-31B	b	Matching
	d	Entity
P13-32B		Net income, $20,000; total assets, $269,000
P13-33B	1a	Increase in cost of goods sold and depreciation
P13-34B	1b	$302,075
	1c	$600,000
P13-35B		Net monetary assets, Dec. 31, 1993, $129,000; Purchasing power loss, $23,496
P13-36B	1	Purchasing power loss, $61,697
PC	1	Net loss, $(13,000)
	1	Total liabilities and owner's equity, $335,000

Chapter 14

E14-13		D. Jones, Capital cr., $21,500
E14-14		Elsie, Capital cr., $55,060
E14-15		S. May, $12,000
E14-16		I. S. You, $30,000
E14-17		G. Henry, $27,000
E14-18	1	J. Galley, capital, $16,000
E14-19		T. George, Capital cr., $20,000
E14-20	2	T. Turner, Capital cr., $60,000
E14-21		A. Nielson, Capital dr., $65,000
E14-22		Liability to Estate of A. Nielson cr., $65,000
E14-23		Cash to Anders, $210,000
E14-24		Cash to Dawson, $17,500
P14-25A	1	H. Iococa, Capital cr., $35,000
	2	H. Iococa, Capital cr., $24,000
	4	H. Iococa, Capital cr., $70,000
P14-26A	1	Income to Badger, $60,000
	3	Income to Badger, $50,000
P14-27A	3	Income to Henry, $14,000
P14-28A	1	Net income, $40,000
	2	Income to Cedar, $22,200
	4	Total assets, $189,000
P14-29A	3	B. Harris, Capital cr., $35,000
	4	B. Harris, Capital cr., $47,000
	6	B. Harris, Capital cr., $60,000
P14-30A	2	Cash payment to Eidson, $66,000
	3	Cash payment to Eidson, $62,000
P14-31A		Cash payment to Sawyer, $40,000
P14-25B	1	A. George, Capital cr., $10,000
	2	A. George, Capital cr., $14,000
	4	A. George, Capital cr., $42,000
P14-26B	1	Income to Burns, $24,000
	3	Income to Burns, $36,250
P14-27B	3	Income to Jordan, $44,000

P14-28B	1	Net income, $109,000
	2	Income to Moline, $59,000
	4	Total assets, $181,000
P14-29B	3	D. Hintz, Capital cr., $47,000
	4	D. Hintz, Capital cr., $40,000
	6	D. Hintz, Capital cr., $56,000
P14-30B	2	Cash payment to Reicher, $80,000
	3	Cash payment to Reicher, $95,000
P14-31B		Cash payment to Haze, $67,500
PC		Apr. 1, 1993, P. Wagner, Capital cr., $52,000; Jan. 1, 1994, J. Wayner, Capital cr., $35,000; 1994 income to Cash, $51,300; Jan. 31, 1995, cash payment to Wayne, $10,500

Chapter 15

E15-15	2	Total stockholders' equity, $795,000
E15-16	1	$500,000
	5	$5
E15-17	1a	60,000 shares
	1b	100,000 shares
	4a	$50
	4b	$8
	5	$240,000
E15-18	1	Paid-in Capital—Excess over Par Value, Common cr., $48,000
	3	Paid-in Capital—Excess over Stated Value cr., $40,000
E15-19		Sep. 2, Common stock cr., $10,000; Paid-in Capital—Excess over Par Value, Common cr., $2,000
		Nov. 11, Paid-in Capital—Excess over Par Value, Common cr., $40,000
E15-20	1	Common Stock cr., $250,000
	3	Paid-in Capital—Excess over Par Value, Common cr., $18,000
E15-21		Sep. 5, Cash dr., $20,000; Subscriptions Receivable—Common dr., $40,000
		Sep. 30, Common Stock Subscribed dr., $20,000
E15-22		Cash collected from stock transactions, $2,682,000
E15-23		Paid-in Capital—Donations cr., $230,000
E15-24		Aug. 7, Paid-in Capital—Excess over Stated Value, Common cr., $200,000
E15-25		Total paid-in capital, $1,050,000
E15-26	d	Paid-in Capital—Excess over Par Value, Preferred cr., $25,000
P15-27A	1	Total capital stock, $600,000
	2a1	$400,000
	2a2	$200,000
P15-28A	2	Common Stock, $650,000; Paid-in Capital—Excess over Par Value, Common, $175,000
P15-29A	3	Total capital stock, $159,000; total paid-in capital, $605,500
P15-30A	4	Total capital stock, $1,519,000; total paid-in capital, $2,289,000
P15-31A	2a	Preferred shares, 5,000; common shares, 25,600
	b	$378,000
P15-32A		Total capital stock, $1,100,000; total stockholders' equity, $2,340,000

Copyright © 1992 by Harcourt Brace Jovanovich, Inc. All rights reserved.

P15-33A	1	$.10 per share
	2	Yes, 550,000 shares
P15-27B	1	Total stockholders' equity, $2,000,000
	2a1	$100,000
	2a2	$400,000
P15-28B	2	Total capital paid-in by stockholders, $1,110,000
P15-29B	3	Total capital stock, $270,000; total paid-in capital, $408,000
P15-30B	4	Total capital stock, $940,000; total stockholders' equity, $2,220,000
P15-31B	2a1	14,000 shares
	2a2	55,000 shares
	2b	$722,500
P15-32B		Total capital stock, $1,300,000; total stockholders' equity, $3,200,000
P15-33B	1	135,333,333 shares
	3	$.525 per share
PC	2	Total assets, $279,400; total capital stock, $143,000

Chapter 16

E16-15	a	Decrease
	h	No effect
	j	No effect
E16-16		Jun. 4, Dividends Payable—Common cr., $30,000
E16-17		Dividend to common stockholders, $84,000
E16-18		Aug. 2, Paid-in Capital—Excess over Par, $390,000
E16-19	1a	Stock Dividends—Common dr., $150,000
	2b	Stock dividend, $750,000; stock split, $600,000
E16-20	c	Treasury Stock—Common cr., $3,600
E16-21		Aug. 30, Paid-in Capital—Excess over Par Value, Common dr., $2,000
E16-22	a	Stock Dividends to Be Issued—Common cr., $15,000
	e	Dividends—Common dr., $11,490
E16-23	1	$1.40
	2	$1.32
E16-24		Total stockholders' equity, $1,770,000
E16-25		Net income, $240,000
E16-26		Earnings per share, $5.60
E16-27		Primary earnings per share, $6.40; fully diluted earnings per share, $5.395
P16-28A	a	Cash dr., $96,000
	g	Stock Dividends to Be Issued—Common cr., $8,000
P16-29A	1d	Paid-in Capital from Treasury Stock Transactions, Common cr., $2,000
	3	Total stockholders' equity, $1,870,100
P16-30A	1b	Paid-in Capital—Excess over Par Value, Common cr., $121,500
	1f	Stock Dividends—Common dr., $69,000
	2	Total stockholders' equity, $616,500
P16-31A	1	Book value per share of common stock, $9
	2	Book value per share of common stock, $8.40
P16-32A	1	Net income, $960,000 (earnings per share, $9.60)
P16-33A		Weighted average common shares outstanding, 45,000
		Earnings per share, $2.82

P16-34A	1	Primary earnings per share, $2.30
	2	Fully diluted earnings per share, $2
P16-28B	a	Common Stock cr., $198,000
	g	Dividends Payable—Preferred dr., $5,250
P16-29B	1d	Treasury Stock—Preferred cr., $36,000
	3	Total stockholders' equity, $1,871,000
P16-30B	1b	Paid-in Capital—Excess over Par Value, Common cr., $195,000
	1f	Stock Dividends—Common dr., $96,000
	2	Total stockholders' equity, $1,047,000
P16-31B	1	Book value per share of common stock, $9.42
	2	Book value per share of common stock, $8.52
P16-32B	1	Net income, $18,000 (earnings per share, $.18)
P16-33B		Weighted average common shares outstanding, 94,000
		Earnings per share, $2.70
P16-34B	1	Primary net loss per share, $(.80)
	2	Fully diluted net loss per share, $(.80)
PC	1	May 9, Accumulated Depreciation dr., $20,000
	1	Oct. 5, Cash dr., $24,000
	2	Total stockholders' equity, $878,550
	3	Book value per share, $7.18

Chapter 17

E17-13	3	Interest Payable cr., $30,000
E17-14	a	Discount
	d	Premium
E17-15	a	$213,008
E17-16	2	Interest Expense dr., $58,000
E17-17	3	Interest Expense dr., $35,628
E17-18	2	Interest Expense dr., $31,250
E17-19	2	Jun. 30, 1994, Interest Expense dr., $113,305
E17-20	d	$392,200
	f	$210,715
E17-21		Interest Expense, $10,000
E17-22	2	Interest Expense, dr., $3,500
E17-23	2	Paid-in Capital—Excess over Par Value, Common cr., $183,200
E17-24		Dec. 31, 1995, bond sinking fund deposit, $40,000
E17-25		Premium bal., $6,800
E17-26		Aug. 1, interest expense, $873.69
P17-27A		Dec. 31, 1993, Interest Expense dr., $16,280
P17-28A		1993 interest expense, $34,650
P17-29A	1	Third-period interest expense, $23,868
P17-30A	1	$384,925; third-period interest expense, $21,303
	2	Dec. 31, 1993, Interest Expense dr., $7,078
P17-31A	2	$442,651
	5	1993 interest expense, $53,212
P17-32A	1b	Original issue price, $291,740
	2	Cash dr., $296,740

P17-33A	1	Dec.1, 1994, Cash dr., $525,000
	3	No gain or loss
P17-27B		Dec. 31, 1993, Interest Expense dr., $20,800
P17-28B		1993 interest expense, $31,680
P17-29B	1	Third-period interest expense, $46,474
P17-30B	1	$481,600
		Third-period interest expense, $29,069
	2	Dec. 31, 1993, Interest Expense dr., $28,980
P17-31B	2	$562,311
	5	1993 interest expense, $56,137
P17-32B	1b	Original issue price, $102,340
	2	Cash dr., $104,340
P17-33B	1	Oct. 1, 1994, Cash dr., $787,500
	3	Gain on retirement, $7,500
PC		Dec. 31, 1993, Interest Expense dr., $46,000
		Jan. 1, 1994, Paid-in Capital—Excess over Par Value, Common cr., $434,000
		Jul. 1, 1994, gain on retirement, $7,250

Chapter 18

E18-13		Dec. 13, Interest Revenue cr., $15,000
E18-14		Dec. 31, Unrealized Loss on Short-term Investments dr., $500
E18-15	2	Feb. 1, 1994, Realized Gain on Short-term Investments cr., $1,900
E18-16		Jan. 1, 1994, Cash dr., $508,900
E18-17		Jul. 11, Dividend Revenue cr., $1,000
E18-18		Nov. 14, Cash dr., $9,000
		Dec. 31, Equity in Investee Income cr., $24,000
E18-19	1a	Dividends Revenue cr., $2,400
	2a	Long-term Investment in Stocks—Sparrow Co. Stock cr., $7,200
E18-20		Dec. 31, 1993, Allowance to Reduce Long-term Investments to Market cr., $4,000
E18-21	b	Dec. 31, Interest Revenue cr., $23,600
E18-22	b	Dec. 31, Interest Revenue cr., $24,200
E18-23		Jun. 30, 1994, Interest Revenue cr., $15,906
E18-24	1	Dec. 31, Interest Receivable dr., $27,500
	2	Feb. 1, Long-term Investments in Bonds—Lincoln Co. cr., $5,067
E18-25	1	Jul. 1, Interest Revenue cr., $12,660
	2	Jul. 1, Interest Revenue cr., $18,990
P18-26A	1	Mar. 31, Unrealized Loss on Short-term Investments dr., $5,000
	2	Total net investment revenue, $10,460
P18-27A		Dec. 31, 1993, Interest Receivable dr., $48,000; Feb. 1, 1994, Realized Gain on Short-term Investments cr., $15,700
P18-28A	1	Nov. 1, Realized Gain on Long-term Investments cr., $7,500; Dec. 31, Unrealized Loss on Long-term Investments dr., $31,000
P18-29A	2	1994, $7,200 dividends revenue by Hiltonic
	3	1993, $240,000; 1995, $200,000; 1997, $200,000
P18-30A	1	Equity method
	2	1993, $48,000; 1995, $42,000; 1997, $22,400

P18-31A		Dec. 31, 1993, Interest Revenue cr., $16,550; Jun. 30, 1994, Cash dr., $17,500
P18-32A		Aug. 1, 1993, Interest Revenue cr., $40,778; Feb. 1, 1994, Long-term Investment in Bonds—CSM Company dr., $137; Dec. 31, 1994, Interest Receivable dr., $33,333
P18-26B	1	Mar. 31, 1994, Unrealized Loss on Short-term Investments dr., $9,800
	2	Total net investment loss, $(10,050)
P18-27B		Dec. 31, 1993, Interest Receivable dr., $42,000
		Mar. 1, 1993, Realized Loss on Short-term Investments dr., $19,300
P18-28B	1	Nov. 1, Realized Gain on Long-term Investments cr., $600
	1	Dec. 31, no entry needed since market value is greater than cost
P18-29B	2	1994, $120 dividend revenue recognized by Elm
	3	1993, $6,000; 1995, $1,000; 1997, $1,000
P18-30B	1	Equity method
	2	1993, $1,200; 1995, $300; 1997, $500
P18-31B		Sep. 30, 1993, Interest Revenue cr., $38,884; Mar. 31, 1994, Interest Receivable cr., $22,500
P18-32B		Sep. 1, 1993, Interest Revenue cr., $25,857; Mar. 1, 1994, Long-term Investment in Bonds—Barny Corp. dr., $302
PC		Nov. 1, Cash cr., $428,000
		Dec. 31, Equity in Investee Income cr., $24,000
		Dec. 31, Unrealized Loss on Short-term Investments dr., $535

Chapter 19

E19-18	c	Financing
	e	No effect
	h	Investing
E19-19	b1	$230,000
	b2	Operating
	g1	$(20,000)
	g2	Financing
E19-20		Net cash provided by operating activities, $21,000
E19-21	a	Cash receipts from customers, $545,000
	b	Cash payments to suppliers, $365,000
E19-22	c	Cash payments to employees, $74,000
	d	Cash payments for rent, $44,000
E19-23		Net income, $62,000
E19-24	2	Net purchases of merchandise, $241,000
	4	Cash payments for operating expenses, $102,000
E19-25	A	Cash provided by operating activities, $15
	C	Cash provided by operating activities, $94
E19-26	1	Net cash provided by operating activities, $1,000
E19-27		Net cash used by investing activities, $(6,000)
E19-28	2	Cash inflow from sale of machinery, $6,000
E19-29	2	Cash inflow of $150,000 from sale of stock
E19-30		Net cash provided by operating activities, $5,000
E19-31		Net cash provided by operating activities, $5,000
P19-32A		Net cash used in operating activities, $(30,000)

P19-33A	1	Net income, $22,000
	2	Net cash used in operating activities $(132,000)
P19-34A	1	Net cash used in operating activities, $(47,000)
P19-35A	1	Net cash used in operating activities, $(88,000)
	1	Cash and cash equivalents at end of year, $22,000
P19-36A	1	Net cash provided by operating activities, $68,000
	1	Cash and cash equivalents at end of year, $115,000
P19-37A	1	Net cash used in operating activities, $(13,000)
	1	Cash and cash equivalents at end of year, $87,000
P19-38A	1	Net cash used in operating activities, $(53,800)
	1	Cash and cash equivalents at end of year, $11,000
P19-32B		Net cash provided by operating activities, $52,000
		Cash and cash equivalents at end of year, $442,000
P19-33B	1	Net income, $15,000
	2	Cash and cash equivalents at end of year, $268,000
P19-34B	1	Net cash provided by operating activities, $160,000
P19-35B	1	Net cash provided by operating activities, $60,000
		Cash and cash equivalents at end of year, $67,000
P19-36B	1	Net cash provided by operating activities, $71,500
		Cash and cash equivalents at end of year, $25,500
P19-37B	1	Net cash used in operating activities, $(8,600)
	1	Cash and cash equivalents at end of year, $39,800
P19-38B	1	Net cash provided by operating activities, $35,000
	1	Cash and cash equivalents at end of year, $39,000
PC	1	Net cash used in operating activities, $(36,000)
	1	Cash and cash equivalents at end of year, $6,000

Chapter 20

E20-16	A	Sales, 29.2%; cost of goods sold, 15.2%
E20-17		Net income; 1993, 119.8%; 1992, 107.1%; 1991, 100%
E20-18		Net income (loss); 1993, 12.5%; 1992, (7.0)%
E20-19		1993; current assets, 26.4%; Investments, 11.1%
E20-20		Favorable, Net income increased by 16% since 1990.
		Unfavorable, Cost of goods sold increased by 28% since 1990.
E20-21	a	1993, 1.89; 1992, 1.75
	c	1993, 12.21 times; 1992, 12.62 times
E20-22	a	1993, 29.9%; 1992, 38.8%
E20-23	b	1993, 2.34 times; 1992, 2.28 times
	d	1993, 32.1%; 1992, 34.9%
E20-24		Net income: 1993, 9.0%; 1992, 8.8%; 1991, 7.7%
E20-25		Total current assets: 1993, 54.7%; 1992, 54.6%
E20-26	a	a, 15 times; b, 3.7%; c, 44.4%
E20-27	a	Circle Video
	b	Square Video
	d	Circle Video
E20-28		No check figure.
P20-29A	1	Total assets, increase, $30,000, 5.5%
	2	Net income, decrease, $(10,500), (15.0)%

P20-30A	1	Total liabilities, 1993, 25.5%; 1992, 28.7%
	2	Net income, 1993; 6.6%; 1992, 9.3%
P20-31A	7	1993, 9.5 times; 1992, 11.0 times
	12	1993, $.595; 1992, $.70
P20-32A	1	Total assets: 1993, $1,140; 1992, $1,320
P20-33A	1a	Total assets: 1993, $870,000; 1992, $780,000
	1b	Net income: 1993, $83,520; 1992, $123,975
P20-34A	7	1993, 8.48 times; 1992, 10.33 times
	12	1993, 16.6 times; 1992, 15.3 times
	13	1993, 2.6%; 1992, 2.7%
P20-35A	3	No effect
	4	Increase
	7	Decrease
P20-29B	1	Total assets, decrease, $(36,000), (4.0)%
	2	Net income, increase, $4,200, 12.0%
P20-30B	1	Total liabilities; 1993, 16.6%; 1992, 21.6%
	2	Net income; 1993, 4.9%; 1992, 3.9%
P20-31B	7	1993, 6.6 times; 1992, 6.0 times
	12	1993, $.392; 1992, $.35
P20-32B	1	Total assets; 1993, $2,720; 1992, $2,360; 1991, $2,000
P20-33B	1a	Current assets; 1993, 27.6%; 1992, 37.5%
	1b	Net income; 1993, 8.7%; 1992, 14.5%
P20-34B	7	1993, 2.91 times; 1992, 2.91 times
	12	1993, 1,766.7 times; 1992, 580 times
	13	1993, 1.8%; 1992, 1.6%
P20-35B		1. Increase; 2. Decrease; 3. No effect
		8. No effect; 9. Increase; 10. Increase
PC	1	Net income: Coca-Cola, 19.2%; Pepsico, 5.9%
	2a	Coca-Cola, 0.99; Pepsico, 0.96
	2c	Coca-Cola, 6.73 times; Pepsico, 3.22 times
	2h	Coca-Cola, 22.8 times; Pepsico, 18.8 times

Chapter 21

E21-14		Companies 1 and 4
E21-15		A lower income tax would result from filing as separate corporations.
E21-16		Gull Point and Warrington Finance Company should be consolidated.
E21-17		Investment in Tyson Company, $0; Retained Earnings, $1,565,000
E21-18		Retained Earnings, $1,565,000; Minority Interest, $250,000
E21-19		Debit accounts, consolidated balance sheet totals, $540,000
E21-20		Credit accounts, consolidated balance sheet totals, $580,000
E21-21		Debit accounts, consolidated balance sheet totals, $540,000
E21-22		Dec. 31, Cash dr. $7,000
E21-23	1	Dec. 31, Equity in Yana Company Income cr., $50,000
	2	Debit accounts, consolidated balance sheet totals, $590,000
E21-24		Credit accounts, consolidated balance sheet totals, $540,530
E21-25		Net income, consolidated income statement, $70,000
E21-26		Jan. 9, 1994, Foreign Currency Exchange Loss dr., $37,500
P21-27A		Retained earnings, consolidated balance sheet, $155,760

P21-28A	1	Debit accounts, consolidated balance sheet, $1,045,000
	2	Total liabilities, $335,000
P21-29A	1	Amount paid over book value, $27,000
	3	Total assets, $1,045,000
P21-30A	1	Dec. 31, Equity in Tom's Import Coffee Income cr., $40,000
	2	Credit accounts, consolidated balance sheet, $1,075,000
P21-31A		Accounts Receivable-General Customers, $296,500
		Accounts Payable—Affiliate, $0
P21-32A		Total revenues, $684,000; net income, $103,000
P21-33A		Dec. 28, Accounts Receivable, Hamburg Company cr., $14,000; Dec. 31, Foreign Currency Exchange Loss dr., $1,000
P21-27B		Retained earnings, consolidated balance sheet, $311,520
P21-28B	1	Debit accounts, consolidated balance sheet, $855,000
	2	Total liabilities, $305,000
P21-29B	1	Amount paid over book value, $38,000
	3	Total assets, $900,000
P21-30B	1	Dec. 31, Equity in Al's Pet Fish Company Income cr., $50,000
	2	Credit accounts, consolidated balance sheet, $899,000
P21-31B		Accounts Receivable—General Customers, $393,000
		Accounts Payable—Affiliate, $0
P21-32B		Total revenues, $757,000; Net income, $47,000
P21-33B		Dec. 29, Cash dr., $51,852
		Dec. 31, Foreign Currency Exchange Loss dr., $2,500
PC	1	Amount paid above book value, $40,000
	2	Debit accounts, consolidated balance sheet, $910,000
	3	Total stockholders' equity, $730,000

Chapter 22

E22-13	a	Product, direct
	f	Product, overhead
E22-14		Net cost of material purchases, $674,000; cost of materials used, $679,000
E22-15	1	Cost of materials available for use, $13,700; returns and allowances, $1,000
E22-16		Current period manufacturing costs, $842,000; cost of goods manufactured, $837,000
E22-17		Cost of goods sold, $990,000
E22-18	1	Cost of goods sold, $32,000
	2	Cost of goods available for sale, $135,000
	3	Gross margin on sales, $11,000
E22-19		Cost of goods manufactured, $1,557,000; cost of goods sold, $1,552,000; Gross margin on sales, $448,000
E22-20	a	Purchases dr., $600,000
	b	Materials Inventory dr., $600,000
E22-21		Manufacturing Overhead Control dr., $8,000
E22-22		Work-in-Process Inventory cr., $1,400,000; Work-in-Process Inventory bal. Jan. 31, 1993, $280,000

E22-23		Finished Goods Inventory dr., $600,000; Cash dr., $800,000; Finished Goods Inventory cr., $500,000
E22-24	a	Total manufacturing costs, $700,000; Cost of goods manufactured, $682,000
	b	Cost of goods sold, $707,000
E22-25		Work-in-Process Inventory, $160,000
E22-26		Net income, $150,000
P22-27A	1	Manufacturing overhead, $59,000; total manufacturing costs, $309,000
	2	Total nonmanufacturing expense, $80,000
	6	Inventoriable costs, $309,000
P22-28A	1	Total manufacturing costs, $125,000; cost of goods manufactured, $124,000
P22-29A	a	Total manufacturing costs, $350,000
	b	Cost of goods sold, $356,000
P22-30A	1	Materials purchased, $307,000
	3	Cost of goods manufactured, $920,000
P22-31A	1	Cost of goods manufactured, $280,000
	2	Gross margin on sales, $306,000
P22-32A	a	Purchased materials on account
	f	Charged $22,000 overhead to work-in-process
P22-33A	3	Total manufacturing costs, $585,000; cost of goods manufactured, $550,000
	4	Net income, $20,000
P22-27B	1	Manufacturing overhead, $227,000
	2	Total nonmanufacturing expenses, $350,000
	6	Inventoriable costs, $787,000
P22-28B		Total costs in process, $437,000; cost of goods manufactured, $413,000
P22-29B	a	Cost of goods manufactured, $694,000
	b	Cost of goods sold, $702,000
P22-30B	1	Materials purchased, $499,000
	2	Manufacturing overhead, $280,000
	3	Current period manufacturing costs, $1,300,000
P22-31B	1	$28 per unit
	2	$108,000
	3	Net loss, $(22,000)
P22-32B	6	Used $11,000 direct materials
	h	Sold products costing $39,000
P22-33B	3	Current period manufacturing costs, $505,000; cost of goods manufactured, $500,000
	4	Gross margin on sales, $310,000
PC	3	Current period manufacturing costs, $53,000; cost of goods manufactured, $44,000

Chapter 23

E23-13		a, b, d, f
E23-14		Materials Inventory dr., $4,000
E23-15		Manufacturing (60%); a. Depreciation, $90,000; b. Utilities, $42,000
E23-16		Work-in-Process Inventory dr., $4,600

E23-17		Work-in-Process Inventory dr., $840; Manufacturing Overhead Control dr., $80
E23-18	a	$18 per direct labor hour
	c	300% of direct materials
E23-19		Job no. C101: Overhead applied, $100; total cost of job, $380
E23-20		Manufacturing Overhead Control dr., $48,600 (to record the incurrence of factory overhead); Work-in-Process Inventory dr., $48,000 (overhead applied)
E23-21		Job no. 137: Direct labor and manufacturing overhead, $9,000; direct labor, $6,000
E23-22	a	$2,800
	c	$12,100
E23-23		Finished Goods Inventory dr., $18,900
E23-24	1	300% of direct material cost
	2	Finished Goods Inventory dr., $91,000
E23-25	1	Manufacturing overhead, $620
	2	Finished Goods Inventory dr., $1,320
E23-26		Manufacturing overhead applied, $420,000
P23-27A	1	Manufacturing: Square footage 55%; miles driven, 15%; no. of employees, 50%
	2	Manufacturing: Rent, $55,000; gas and oil expense, $3,000; cafeteria, $25,000
P23-28A	1a	$10 per direct labor hour
	1b	200%
	1c	300%
P23-29A	1, 2	Overhead application rate, $16 per direct labor hour; total overhead applied during January, $64,000
	3	Underapplied manufacturing overhead, $800
P23-30A	1	Manufacturing overhead, $560
	2	$165 per receiver
P23-31A	b	Salaries and Wages Payable cr., $78,000
	e	i. Cost of Goods Sold dr., $60,000; ii. Sales cr., $85,000
P23-32A	1	Total material issued, $38,000; materials inventory Aug. 31, 1993, $22,000
	4	Job 85 only, $83,400
P23-33A	4	Work-in-process inventory, Job 92 only, $51,000
	5	Overhead incurred, $38,000
P23-27B	1	Printing: Square footage, 50%; Hours of service, 20%; Number of employees, 30%
	2	Printing: Building-related, $100,000; accounting and data processing, $16,000; health club, $45,000
P23-28B	1	a. $6 per pound of direct material; b. 125% of direct labor cost; c. $10 per direct labor hour
P23-29B	1, 2	Overhead application rate, 200% of direct labor cost; total overhead applied, $124,000
	3	Underapplied manufacturing overhead, $1,500
P23-30B	1	Manufacturing overhead, $550
	2	$430

P23-31B		Manufacturing Overhead Control cr., $200,000 (application of overhead for February)
P23-32B	1	$40,000
	2	$41,500
	3	$4,900
	4	$19,300
P23-33B	4	Work-in-Process Inventory, $75,000 (Job 285 only); finished goods inventory $39,000 (Job 286 only)
	5	Underapplied overhead, $1,500
PC	1	$2 per machine hour
	4	Overapplied, $1,500
	5	Gross margin on sales, $13,000; net loss, $4,000
	6	Work-in-process inventory, $134,000

Chapter 24

E24-15		a, c, e
E24-16		Total quantity to be accounted for, 15,000 units
E24-17		Total quantity to be accounted for, 49,500 units
E24-18		Materials, 800 units
E24-19		Direct labor, 4,800 units; manufacturing overhead, 4,800 units
E24-20		FIFO: Materials, total equivalent units, 40,000; Weighted average: Labor and overhead, total equivalent units, 44,600
E24-21		$204,000
E24-22		Prior department costs, $4 per unit; labor costs, $11 per unit
E24-23		$23,000
E24-24		Materials, total equivalent units, 25,000; labor unit cost, $3 per unit; costs transferred to finished goods department, $273,000
E24-25		FIFO: Labor and overhead, total equivalent units, 58,200; labor unit costs, $3.50 per unit; total costs transferred to next department, $509,720. Weighted average: Labor and overhead, total equivalent units, 59,800; Labor unit costs, $3.457 per unit
E24-26		$100,500
E24-27		Products transferred in: Work-in-Process—Shaping cr., $435,000; Products transferred out: Work-in-Process—Packing dr., $390,000
E24-28		Split costs: Product A, $12,000; Product B, $6,000
P24-29A	1	Quantity to be accounted for, 95,000 units
	2	Total equivalent units, 87,000
	3	Unit costs: Materials, $.45 per unit
P24-30A	1	Unit costs: Labor, $.50 per unit; Cost of units transferred, $230,000
	2	$27,000
P24-31A	1	Unit costs: Prior department, $1 per unit; overhead, $.30 per unit. Cost of units transferred to finished goods inventory, $160,000
	2	$12,060
P24-32A		Quantity accounted for, 100,000 units; materials, costs per equivalent unit, $3; total costs accounted for, $959,400
P24-33A		Quantity accounted for, 220,000 units; labor and overhead, equivalent units, 188,000; total costs accounted for, $119,880

P24-34A	1	950,000 units
	2	Equivalent units: Formulating Department, total for materials, labor and overhead, 980,000 units; Packaging Department, materials, 894,000 units, labor and overhead, 910,000 units
	3	Total costs transferred out, $760,000; cost per unit, $.80
	4	$1,527,200
	5	Cost of ending work-in-process: Formulating Department, $72,000; Packaging Department, $209,000
P24-35A		Quantity accounted for, 39,000 units; equivalent units, prior department, 30,000; cost per equivalent unit, prior department, $20; total costs to be accounted for, $1,800,000
P24-36A	1	Split costs: Slim, $14,000; None, $28,000
	2	Total product costs: Slim $40,000; None $48,000
P24-37A	1	Quantity accounted for, 95,000 units
	2	Equivalent units, 91,000
	3	Cost per equivalent unit: Materials, $.45
P24-38A		Materials: Equivalent units for Aug., 230,000 units; costs per equivalent unit, $1.15
	1	$230,000
	2	Total cost of ending inventory, $27,000
P24-39A		Labor and overhead: Total equivalent units, 65,800; unit costs, labor, $.40; overhead, $.30
	1	$160,000
	2	Total cost of work-in-process inventory, Apr. 30, $12,060
P24-40A		Quantity to be accounted for, 100,000 units. Materials: Equivalent units for October, 99,000 units; costs incurred during Oct., $297,000; cost per equivalent unit, $3. Total costs accounted for, $959,400
P24-41A		Quantity to be accounted for, 220,000 units. Materials: Equivalent units, 214,000 units; cost per equivalent unit, $.290
P24-42A	1	950,000 units
	2	Equivalent units: Formulating Department, 1,040,000 units; Packaging Department, materials, 1,010,000 units
	3	$.80
	4	Weighted average cost per equivalent unit, Packaging Department, $1.68
	5	Total cost of work-in-process, Mar. 31: Formulating Department, $72,000; Packaging Department, $206,000
P24-29B	1	Quantity accounted for, 570,000 units
	2	Total equivalent units, 498,000
	3	Materials, $.10; Labor, $.06; Overhead, $.04
P24-30B		Materials: Equivalent units, 809,000 units; unit costs, $.10
	1	$320,000
	2	$1,800
P24-31B	1	Materials, total equivalent units, 360,000; prior department unit cost, $6 per unit; total costs transferred out, $4,200,000
	2	$408,000
P24-32B		Quantity accounted for, 20,000 units; materials, equivalent units for November, 20,000 units; total costs to be accounted for, $791,000; total cost per equivalent unit, $40

P24-33B		Quantity accounted for, 68,000 units; materials, equivalent units for May, 60,400 units; total costs to be accounted for, $3,580,550; total cost per equivalent unit, $55
P24-34B	1	Equivalent units: materials, 45,000 units; labor and overhead, 45,700 units
	2	Labor, $3 per unit; total costs transferred, $460,000
	3	Total equivalent units: prior department, 46,000 units
	4	$504,000
	5	Production, $32,500; Painting, $41,600
P24-35B		Electronics Department: Quantity accounted for, 24,000 units; materials, equivalent units for May, 24,000 units; total costs to be accounted for, $291,000; total cost per equivalent unit, $13.
		Casing Department: Quantity accounted for, 21,000 units; materials, equivalent units for May, 18,000 units; total costs to be accounted for, $362,100; total cost per equivalent unit, $17.50
P24-36B	1	Split costs: Yellow, $28,000; Red, $7,000
	2	Unit cost: Yellow $1.75; Red, $.75
P24-37B	1	Quantity accounted for, 570,000 units
	2	Equivalent units for Oct., 540,000 units
	3	Labor, $.06; overhead, $.04
P24-38B		Materials: Equivalent units, 809,000 units; unit costs, $.10; units completed and transferred, $320,000; ending work-in-process, $1,800
P24-39B	1	Materials: Total equivalent units, 360,000; prior department unit cost, $6 per unit; total costs transferred out, $4,200,000
	2	Total cost of work-in-process inventory, $408,000
P24-40B		Quantity accounted for, 20,000 units; materials, equivalent units for Nov., 20,000 units; total costs to be accounted for, $791,000; total cost per equivalent unit, $40
P24-41B		Quantity accounted for, 68,000 units; materials, equivalent units for May, 66,000 units; total costs to be accounted for, $3,580,550; total cost per equivalent unit, $54.55
P24-42B	1	Equivalent units: materials, 51,000 units; labor and overhead, 47,500 units
	2	Labor, $3 per unit; Total costs transferred, $460,000
	4	$504,000
	5	Production, $32,500; Painting, $41,600
PC	1	Cutting Department: Quantity accounted for, 900 units; materials, equivalent units for Apr., 800 units; total costs to be accounted for, $15,330; total cost per equivalent unit, $18.
		Sewing Department: Quantity accounted for, 750 units; prior department, equivalent units for Apr., 700 units; total costs to be accounted for, $31,058; total cost per equivalent unit, $43.40
PC for App. 24A	1	Cutting Department: Quantity accounted for, 900 units; materials, equivalent units for Apr., 900 units; total costs to be accounted for, $15,330; total cost per equivalent unit, $17.92
		Sewing Department: Quantity accounted for, 750 units; prior department, equivalent units for Apr., 750 units; total costs to be accounted for, $31,072; total cost per equivalent unit, $43.039

Chapter 25

E25-15		Unit contribution margin, $28; contribution margin percent, 70%
E25-16	a	$7
	d	$500,000
E25-17		$16,000
E25-18		Dollar sales, $180,000; margin of safety, $80,000
E25-19		$30,000
E25-20		Sales budget Nov. totals: Units, 21,600; dollars $1,688,000
E25-21		Total sales in units: Product A, 39,500; Product B, 43,300
E25-22		Production requirement: Jan., 5,800 units
E25-23		Materials purchases: Jun., $89,000
E25-24		Direct labor cost, $6,000,000
E25-25		Ending cash bal.: Jan., $15,000
E25-26A	1	30,000 units
	4	$608,000
P25-27A	1	55,000 units
	3	60,000 units
P25-28A	1a	$8
	1b	$10
	3a	45,000 units
	3b	75,000 units
P25-29A	1	Total sales, quarter 1: 44,500 units
	2	Production requirements, quarter 1: 43,900 units
P25-30A	1	Production requirements, second quarter, 40,500 units
	2	Materials purchases, second quarter: 81,000 units; $40,500
	3	Direct labor, second quarter: 20,250 hours; $121,500
	4	Variable manufacturing overhead, second quarter, $60,750
P25-31A		Total cash receipts for Oct., $84,600
P25-32A	1	Apr.: Total cash available, $120,000; ending bal., $27,900
P25-26B	1	$480,000
	2	$900,000
P25-27B	1	17,000 units
	3	25,000 units
P25-28B	1	1992: Contribution margin, $25; break-even point, 6,000 units
	2	8,334 units
	3	Selling price, $61.72 (rounded)
P25-29B	1	Quarter 1: Total unit sales, 22,800; total dollar sales, $173,000
	2	Quarter 1: Production requirement, 6,600 units
P25-30B	1	Production requirement, quarter 1: 22,000 units
	2	Materials purchases, quarter 1: 88,000 units; $176,000
	3	Direct labor, quarter 1: 5,500 hours; $66,000
	4	Variable manufacturing overhead, quarter 1: $66,000
P25-31B		Nov.: Total cash payments, $212,000
P25-32B	1	Jul.: Total cash available, $157,600; ending bal. $80,600

PC	1	Aug. break-even, 3,000 units
	3	5,543 units
	4	Jul.: Production requirement, 7,200 units; materials purchases, $76,000; Total direct labor cost, $21,600; total manufacturing overhead, $147,600; Total operating expense, $61,000
	5	Total cash available, $474,000; ending cash bal., $42,800

Chapter 26

E26-17		110%: Total variable costs, $825,000; total fixed costs, $600,000
E26-18		Unfavorable, $8,000
E26-19		Unfavorable, $3,000
E26-20		200 lengths
E26-21		1/12 direct labor hours per unit
E26-22		$6 per direct labor hour; $1.50 per unit
E26-23	3	Total standard overhead rate, $18 per direct labor hour
E26-24		$60,000
E26-25		$405,000
E26-26		Materials purchase price variance, $1,400 F
E26-27		Wage rate variance, $375 F; Labor efficiency variance, $160 U
E26-28		Adjusted budget, $4,060,000
E26-29		$6,000 budget variance for overhead
P26-30A		90,000 meals: Total variable expenses, $460,800
P26-31A	1	Variable costs for adjusted budget, $22,375
P26-32A	1	$5.90 per piece
	2	2.10 per leg
	3	Purchase price variance: Plastic, $30,300 F, Materials quantity variance: Legs, $9,600 U
	4	Work-in-Process Inventory dr., $4,200,000
P26-33A	1	Labor rate variance, $1,275 favorable
	2	Work-in-Process Cutting Department dr., $31,200
P26-34A	1	Standard variable overhead rate, $.10 per direct labor hour
	2	Overhead budget adjusted to standard hours, $61,000; overhead volume variance, $500 F
P26-35A	1	Total overhead rate, $4.95 per direct labor hour
	3	Budget variance, $2,400 U
	5	Overhead overapplied, $6,400
P26-36A	1a	$2,400 F
	1c	$4,400 U
	1g	$700 F
	4	Total standard cost, $10 per bucket
P26-30B	1&2	950,000 units: Total expenses, $596,125; total costs per unit, $.6275
P26-31B	1	Adjusted budget: Total variable costs, $49,680; total fixed costs, $11,000; total variance, $2,160 U
P26-32B	1	Purchase price variance: Fabric, $4,500 F; Materials quantity variance: Foam, $1,200 U
P26-33B	1	Variance, total direct labor, $5,550 U
	2	Work-in-Process—Packing Department dr., $48,000

P26-34B	1	Total standard overhead rate, $4 per direct labor hour
	2	Overhead budget variance, $5,300 U
P26-35B		Overhead volume variance, $10,000 U
P26-36B	1a	$7,500 F
	1d	$13,100 F
	1e	$4,100 F
	1f	$9,000 F
	1i	$600 F
	2	Work-in-Process Inventory dr., $92,000; Materials Quantity Variance dr., $4,000; Materials Inventory cr., $92,000
PC	1	90%: Total variable manufacturing overhead, $5,400
	2	Total adjusted budget, $16,300
	3	Total standard cost, $24 per unit
	4	Variances: Materials quantity, $400 U; labor rate, $550 U; Overhead budget, $600 U

Mini Practice Set III

	1	Allocated to manufacturing, $372,000
	2	140%
	3	Work-in-Process Inventory bal., $247,200
	4	Net income, $211,000
	5b	50,275 tires
	6	Total at 45,000 units, $745,000
	7	Materials quantity variance, $10,000 U; Labor efficiency variance, $14,000 F; Overhead volume variance, $0

Chapter 27

E27-14	a	$15.50
	b	$10.50
E27-15	a	$287,000
	b	$220,500
E27-16	a	$52,000
	b	$44,000
E27-17		Jul., $14.40 per unit
E27-18	a	Gross margin, $200,000; net income $117,500
	b	Contribution margin, $350,000; net income, $117,500
E27-19	a	Gross margin, $184,000; net income $104,500
	b	Contribution margin, $322,000; net income, $89,500
E27-21		Total costs variance, $350 U
E27-22		Coffee shop segment margin variance, $2,400 F
E27-23		College Division, segment margin, $39,000
E27-24		Division A, average assets employed, $200,000
P27-26A	1a	$384,000
	1b	$204,000
P27-27A	1	Apr.: a. $19 b. $23
	2a	Net income, $52,000
	2b	Net income, $56,000

P27-28A	1	$12; 60%
	2	$24,000 increase
P27-29A	1	Total expenses, adjusted budget, $191,800; total expenses, variance, $5,950 U
P27-30A	1	Segment margins: Power, $150,000; Sail $195,000
	2	Sail, 45%
P27-31A	1	Return on investment, Grapefruit, 15%
	2	Orange, $54,600
P27-32A	1	Transfer, net loss $(65,000)
	3	Minimum transfer price, $13
P27-26B	1a	$665,000
	2b	$418,500
	3a	$66,500
P27-27B	1	Sept.: a. $8; b. $10.80
	2a	Gross margin on sales, $120,400
	2b	Contribution margin, $165,000
P27-28B	1	$14
	2	4,500 units
	3	Net income, $8,000
	5	$7,000
P27-29B	1	Adjusted budget total costs: Market research, $10,900; advertising, $14,400
	2	Total variance, $2,370 F
P27-30B	1	Contribution margin: Softwoods, $200,000; Company total net income, $80,000
P27-31B	1	Return on investment, Slide, 20%
	2	Residual income, Swing, $120,000
	3	Return on investment, Swing, 28%
P27-32B	1	Contribution margin: Transfer, $34,000; sale outside, $44,000
	3	$18
PC	1	Variable costing, $25; absorption costing, $33
	2	Variable costing: Contribution margin, $114,000; Absorption costing: Gross margin, Net income, $50,400
	4	Segment margin, $58,000
	5	Return on investment, 14.5%; residual income, $(2,000)
	6	$28

Chapter 28

E28-15		Total relevant and differential costs, $28,000
E28-16		Total differential cost, $610,000
E28-17		Total cost to make, $250,000
E28-18		Variable costs, $15,000
E28-19		Total differential costs, $120,000
E28-20	a	$176,000
	b	$44,000
E28-21		3 years
E28-22		3 years

E28-23	a	20%
	b	40%
E28-24		Cash flows, year 4, $8,500
E28-25		Total present value of inflows, $202,854
E28-26		Present value of inflows, Machine A, $208,946
E28-27		After-tax cash flow, $6,500
P28-28A	1	Total costs and expenses, $4,740,000
	2	Variable manufacturing costs, $2,400,000
	3	Increase in income, $210,000
P28-29A	1&2	Total cost to make: With fixed costs, $310,000; with rented facilities, $340,000
P29-30A	2	Increase in contribution margin, $21,600; increase in expenses, $18,800
P28-31A	1&2	Total differential costs if assembled, for 4,000 units, $480,000
P28-32A		Year 2 (1994), Net cash flow, $5,300
P28-33A	1	3 years
	3	26.7%
	5	1.09143
P28-34A	1	3 years
	2	Net present value, $(3,779)
	3	0.973
P28-35A	1	After-tax cash saving, $37,500
	3	Profitability index, 1.0314
P28-28B		Differential costs, $3,290,000
P28-29B	1	Total costs to make, $203,000
	2	Total costs to make, $241,000
P28-30B	1	Department B contribution margin, $2,900
	2	Total net income, Departments A and C, $5,300
P28-31B	1	Total differential costs if 50,000 gallons bottled and labeled, $35,800
P28-32B		Year 3: Net cash flow, $23,200; taxable income, $16,000
P28-33B	1	4.16 years
	2	15%
	4	$19,098
P28-34B	1	Total cash revenue, years 1, 2, and 3, $2,000,000
	2	Present value, 1994, $520,212
	3	Net present value, $(77,560)
	4	Profitability index, West Coast expansion, 1.068
P28-35B	1	Annual income tax increase, $28,000; after-tax annual cash inflow, $72,000
	2	4.3056 years
	3	Profitability index, 1.229
PC	1	Cost to make: Year 2, present value, $(11,110); net present value, $(94,634).

Appendix A

PA-1	Adjusted gross income, $47,000
PA-2	Taxable income, $56,400
PA-3	Taxable income, $52,455
PA-4	Corporate tax for 1988, $190,060

PA-5	1	1991 Net income, $354,997
	2	1991 Net income, $346,500

Appendix C

EC-9	1	b
EC-10	1	$15,861.08
EC-11	1	$15,868.36
EC-12		$10,217.86
EC-13	a	$7,581.57
EC-14		$51,274.20
EC-15	1	$219.59
EC-16		$10,104.38
EC-17		$31,838
EC-18	2	$2,925.45
EC-19		$47,877.69
EC-20		$24,576.42
EC-21		$26,347.51
EC-22		$12,018.24
EC-23		$12,519.84
EC-24		$226,926
EC-25		$837
PC-1	1c	$6,232.43
PC-2	c	$12,833.75

CL-31

CHAPTER 1
An Accounting Information System

EXERCISES

E1-17 Users of Accounting Information

1. _____
_____

2. _____
_____

3. _____
_____

4. _____
_____

5. _____
_____

6. _____
_____

7. _____
_____

8. _____
_____
_____
_____
_____
_____
_____

E1-18 Entity Concept

_____
_____
_____
_____
_____
_____
_____

E1-19 The Accounting Equation

1. Owner's equity: _____

2. Total assets: _____

3. Total liabilities: _____

E1-20 The Accounting Equation

1. Owner's equity: _____

2. Current liabilities: _____

3. Current assets: _____

4. Property, plant, and equipment: _____

5. Long-term liabilities: _____

E1-21 Changes in the Accounting Equation

a. A decrease in an asset, an increase in a liability, or an increase in owner's equity. _____

b. _____

c. _____

d. _____

e. _____

E1-22 Using the Accounting Equation to Analyze a Transaction

_____
_____
_____
_____
_____
_____
_____
_____
_____
_____

E1-23 Using the Accounting Equation to Analyze a Transaction

_____
_____
_____
_____
_____
_____
_____
_____
_____

E1-24 Analysis of Balance Sheet Transactions

Date	Effect on Accounting Equation	ASSETS			=	LIABILITIES	+	OWNER'S EQUITY	Explanation of Change in Owner's Equity
		Cash	+ Office Supplies	+ Truck	=	Accounts Payable	+	P. Anders, Capital	

1-4

E1-25 Analysis of Revenue and Expense Transactions

Date	Effect on Accounting Equation		Cash	+	Accounts Receivable	=	Accounts Payable	+	J. Light, Capital	Explanation of Change in Owner's Equity

ASSETS = LIABILITIES + OWNER'S EQUITY

E1-26 Balance Sheet Classification

a. _____   g. _____

b. _____   h. _____

c. _____   i. _____

d. _____   j. _____

e. _____   k. _____

f. _____

E1-27 Preparation of a Balance Sheet

Balance Sheet

Assets												
Current Assets												
Property, plant, and equipment												
Liabilities												
Current liabilities												
Long-term liabilities												
Owner's Equity												

A AND B PROBLEMS

P1-29A or P1-29B Identifying Accounting Entities

_____
_____
_____
_____
_____
_____
_____
_____
_____
_____
_____
_____
_____
_____
_____
_____
_____
_____
_____

P1-35A or P1-35B The Accounting Equation and the Financial Statements

Requirement 1

Requirement 2

Requirement 3

Requirement 4

PRACTICE CASE

Analyzing Transactions and Preparing Financial Statements

Requirement 1

_____
_____
_____
_____
_____
_____
_____
_____
_____
_____

[See the following pages for Practice Case Requirements 2-4.]

Practice Case (continued)

Requirements 2 and 3

Date	Effect on Accounting Equation	ASSETS	=	LIABILITIES	+	OWNER'S EQUITY	Explanation of Change in Owner's Equity

(continued)

Practice Case Requirements 2 and 3 (continued)

Date	Effect on Accounting Equation	ASSETS	=	LIABILITIES	+	OWNER'S EQUITY	Explanation of Change in Owner's Equity

Practice Case

Requirement 4

a.

Income Statement

b.

Statement of Owner's Equity

1-26

Practice Case Requirement 4 (continued)

c.

_____

Balance Sheet

_____

Practice Case Requirement 4 (continued)

d.

Statement of Cash Flows

Name _____

Section _____

BUSINESS DECISION AND COMMUNICATION PROBLEM

Comparing Balance Sheets to Make a Loan Decision

ETHICAL DILEMMA

Ethics in Recording Transactions

_____
_____
_____
_____
_____
_____
_____
_____
_____
_____
_____
_____
_____
_____
_____
_____
_____
_____
_____
_____
_____
_____
_____
_____
_____
_____
_____
_____
_____
_____
_____
_____
_____
_____
_____
_____
_____
_____
_____
_____
_____
_____

CHAPTER 2
Processing Business Transactions

EXERCISES
E2-16 Setting up a Chart of Accounts

_____

_____

_____

_____

_____

_____

_____

_____

_____

_____

_____

_____

_____

_____

_____

_____

_____

_____

_____

_____

_____

_____

_____

_____

_____

_____

_____

_____

_____

_____

_____

_____

E2-17 Rules of Debit and Credit

1.	7.
2.	8.
3.	9.
4.	10.
5	11.
6.	12.

E2-18 Recording Transactions in the Accounts

E2-19 Analyzing Transactions with T Accounts

Cash

Office Supplies

E2-19 (continued)

Office Furniture	Accounts Payable

Service Revenuc	Advertising Revenue

E2-20 Analysis of Transactions

(continued)

E2-20 (continued)

E2-21 Journalizing Transactions

GENERAL JOURNAL

Date	Accounts and Explanations	PR	Debit	Credit

E2-22 Posting Transactions

GENERAL LEDGER

Cash
Acct. No. __101__

Date	Explanation	PR	Debit	Credit	Balance Debit	Balance Credit

Accounts Payable
Acct. No. __201__

Date	Explanation	PR	Debit	Credit	Balance Debit	Balance Credit

Advertising Expense
Acct. No. __616__

Date	Explanation	PR	Debit	Credit	Balance Debit	Balance Credit

Repair Expense
Acct. No. __723__

Date	Explanation	PR	Debit	Credit	Balance Debit	Balance Credit

Name _____

Section _____

E2-23 Preparing a Trial Balance

Trial Balance

Acct. No.	Account Title	Debits	Credits

E2-24 Effect of Errors on Trial Balance

Error	Would the December 31, 1990, trial balance be out of balance?		If yes, by how much?	Which would be larger?	
	Yes	No		Debit Total	Credit Total
a.					
b.					
c.					
d.					

2-7

E2-25 Identifying the Financial Statements on Which Trial Balance Amounts Appear

a. _____   h. _____

b. _____   i. _____

c. _____   j. _____

d. _____   k. _____

e. _____   l. _____

f. _____   m. _____

g. _____   n. _____

E2-26 Correcting an Income Statement

Income Statement

E2-27 Preparing Financial Statements from a Trial Balance

Income Statement

Statement of Owner's Equity

E2-27 (continued)

Balance Sheet

P2-33A or P2-33B Preparing Financial Statements from Incomplete Data

Requirement 1

Income Statement

Requirement 2

Statement of Owner's Equity

Name _____

Section _____

P2-33A or P2-33B (continued)

Requirement 3

Balance Sheet

Name _____

Section _____

P2-34A Preparing an Income Statement for Southwestern Bell Corporation

Requirement 1

<u>Income Statement</u>

Requirement 2

_____

_____

_____

_____

_____

Requirement 3

_____

_____

_____

_____

_____

P2-34B Determining Total Expenses for Maytag Corporation

Requirement 1

	1989	1988	1987	1986	1985

Requirement 2

Requirement 3

(continued)

P2-34B Requirement 3 (continued)

PRACTICE CASE

Processing Business Transactions

Requirement 1

_____

_____

_____

_____

_____

_____

_____

_____

_____

_____

_____

_____

_____

_____

_____

_____

_____

_____

_____

_____

_____

_____

_____

_____

_____

_____

_____

_____

_____

_____

_____

_____

_____

_____

_____

_____

_____

_____

_____

_____

_____

_____

_____

_____

Practice Case (continued)

Requirements 2 and 4

[Practice Case Requirement 3 is on page 2-44.]

GENERAL LEDGER
Cash   Acct. No. _____

Date	Explanation	PR	Debit	Credit	Balance Debit	Balance Credit

_____   Acct. No. _____

Date	Explanation	PR	Debit	Credit	Balance Debit	Balance Credit

Practice Case Requirements 2 and 4 (continued)

GENERAL LEDGER

_____ Acct. No. _____

Date	Explanation	PR	Debit	Credit	Balance	
					Debit	Credit

_____ Acct. No. _____

Date	Explanation	PR	Debit	Credit	Balance	
					Debit	Credit

_____ Acct. No. _____

Date	Explanation	PR	Debit	Credit	Balance	
					Debit	Credit

_____ Acct. No. _____

Date	Explanation	PR	Debit	Credit	Balance	
					Debit	Credit

Practice Case Requirements 2 and 4 (continued)
GENERAL LEDGER

_____ Acct. No. _____

Date	Explanation	PR	Debit	Credit	Balance	
					Debit	Credit

_____ Acct. No. _____

Date	Explanation	PR	Debit	Credit	Balance	
					Debit	Credit

_____ Acct. No. _____

Date	Explanation	PR	Debit	Credit	Balance	
					Debit	Credit

_____ Acct. No. _____

Date	Explanation	PR	Debit	Credit	Balance	
					Debit	Credit

Practice Case Requirements 2 and 4 (continued)

GENERAL LEDGER

_____ Acct. No. _____

Date	Explanation	PR	Debit	Credit	Balance Debit	Balance Credit

_____ Acct. No. _____

Date	Explanation	PR	Debit	Credit	Balance Debit	Balance Credit

Practice Case (continued)

Requirement 3

GENERAL JOURNAL   Page _____

Date	Accounts and Explanations	PR	Debit	Credit

Practice Case Requirement 3 (continued)

GENERAL JOURNAL

Page _____

Date	Accounts and Explanations	PR	Debit	Credit

2-45

Practice Case (continued)

Requirement 5

Trial Balance

Acct. No.	Account Title	Debits	Credits

Requirement 6

Income Statement

Practice Case Requirement 6 (continued)

Statement of Owner's Equity

Balance Sheet

Name _____

Section _____

BUSINESS DECISION AND COMMUNICATION PROBLEM

Commenting on a Chart of Accounts

_____
_____
_____
_____
_____
_____
_____
_____
_____
_____
_____
_____
_____
_____
_____
_____
_____
_____
_____
_____
_____
_____
_____
_____
_____
_____
_____
_____
_____
_____
_____
_____
_____
_____
_____
_____
_____
_____
_____
_____
_____
_____

(continued)

Name _____

Section _____

Business Decision and Communication Problem (continued)

ETHICAL DILEMMA

Neglecting to Record Expenses

_____
_____
_____
_____
_____
_____
_____
_____
_____
_____
_____
_____
_____
_____
_____
_____
_____
_____
_____
_____
_____
_____
_____
_____
_____
_____
_____
_____
_____
_____
_____
_____
_____
_____
_____
_____
_____
_____
_____
_____
_____
_____
_____
_____
_____
_____
_____

CHAPTER 3
Adjusting Entries

EXERCISES

E3-12 Applying the Matching Principle

E3-13 Prepaid Expense Adjustment

E3-13 (continued)

GENERAL JOURNAL

Page _____

Date	Accounts and Explanations	PR	Debit	Credit

E3-14 Prepaid Expense Adjustments

GENERAL JOURNAL

Page _____

Date	Accounts and Explanations	PR	Debit	Credit

E3-15 Depreciation Adjustment

Requirement 1

_____
_____
_____
_____
_____
_____
_____
_____

Requirements 2 and 3

_____
_____
_____
_____
_____
_____
_____
_____
_____
_____
_____

Requirement 4

_____
_____
_____
_____
_____
_____
_____
_____
_____
_____
_____
_____
_____

E3-16 Adjustment for Unearned Revenue

Requirement 1

GENERAL JOURNAL

Page _____

Date	Accounts and Explanations	PR	Debit	Credit

Requirement 2

_____

_____

_____

_____

_____

_____

_____

_____

_____

_____

E3-17 Accrued Expense Adjustment

GENERAL JOURNAL

Page _____

Date	Accounts and Explanations	PR	Debit	Credit

E3-18 Accrued Revenue Adjustment

GENERAL JOURNAL

Page _____

Date	Accounts and Explanations	PR	Debit	Credit

E3-19 Various Accrual Adjustments

GENERAL JOURNAL

Page _____

Date	Accounts and Explanations	PR	Debit	Credit

E3-20 Various Adjustments

GENERAL JOURNAL

Date	Accounts and Explanations	PR	Debit	Credit

Name _____

Section _____

E3-21 Various Adjustments

Requirement 1

GENERAL JOURNAL

Page _____

Date	Accounts and Explanations	PR	Debit	Credit

E3-22 Calculation of Information from Adjustment Data

Requirement 1

_____
_____
_____
_____
_____
_____
_____
_____
_____
_____
_____
_____
_____
_____
_____
_____
_____

Requirement 2

_____
_____
_____
_____
_____
_____
_____
_____
_____
_____
_____
_____
_____
_____
_____
_____
_____
_____

E3-23 (Appendix) Alternative Approaches of Accounting for Prepaid Expense

Case 1

GENERAL JOURNAL

Page _____

Date	Accounts and Explanations	PR	Debit	Credit

Case 2

GENERAL JOURNAL

Page _____

Date	Accounts and Explanations	PR	Debit	Credit

E3-24 (Appendix) Alternative Approaches of Accounting for Unearned Revenue

Requirement 1

GENERAL JOURNAL

Page _____

Date	Accounts and Explanations	PR	Debit	Credit

Requirement 2

_____

_____

_____

_____

_____

Requirement 3

GENERAL JOURNAL

Page _____

Date	Accounts and Explanations	PR	Debit	Credit

A AND B PROBLEMS

P3-25A or P3-25B Analyzing Adjustments

a.

Date	Accounts and Explanations	PR	Debit	Credit

GENERAL JOURNAL Page _____

Date	Accounts and Explanations	PR	Debit	Credit

b.

3-11

P3-25A or P3-25B Requirement b (continued)

_____
_____
_____
_____
_____
_____
_____

GENERAL JOURNAL

Page _____

Date	Accounts and Explanations	PR	Debit	Credit

c.

_____
_____
_____
_____
_____
_____
_____

P3-25A or P3-25B Requirement c (continued)

GENERAL JOURNAL

Page _____

Date	Accounts and Explanations	PR	Debit	Credit

d.

P3-25A or P3-25B Requirement d (continued)

GENERAL JOURNAL

Date	Accounts and Explanations	PR	Debit	Credit

e.

GENERAL JOURNAL

Date	Accounts and Explanations	PR	Debit	Credit

P3-25B

f.

GENERAL JOURNAL

Date	Accounts and Explanations	PR	Debit	Credit

P3-26A or P3-26B Adjusting Entries from a Trial Balance and Added Data

Requirement 1

GENERAL LEDGER

_____   Acct. No. _____

Date	Explanation	PR	Debit	Credit	Balance	
					Debit	**Credit**

_____   Acct. No. _____

Date	Explanation	PR	Debit	Credit	Balance	
					Debit	**Credit**

_____   Acct. No. _____

Date	Explanation	PR	Debit	Credit	Balance	
					Debit	**Credit**

_____   Acct. No. _____

Date	Explanation	PR	Debit	Credit	Balance	
					Debit	**Credit**

P3-26A or P3-26B Requirement 1 (continued)

GENERAL LEDGER

_____ Acct. No. _____

Date	Explanation	PR	Debit	Credit	Balance	
					Debit	Credit

_____ Acct. No. _____

Date	Explanation	PR	Debit	Credit	Balance	
					Debit	Credit

_____ Acct. No. _____

Date	Explanation	PR	Debit	Credit	Balance	
					Debit	Credit

_____ Acct. No. _____

Date	Explanation	PR	Debit	Credit	Balance	
					Debit	Credit

P3-26A or P3-26B Requirement 1 (continued)

GENERAL LEDGER

_____ Acct. No. _____

Date	Explanation	PR	Debit	Credit	Balance	
					Debit	Credit

_____ Acct. No. _____

Date	Explanation	PR	Debit	Credit	Balance	
					Debit	Credit

_____ Acct. No. _____

Date	Explanation	PR	Debit	Credit	Balance	
					Debit	Credit

_____ Acct. No. _____

Date	Explanation	PR	Debit	Credit	Balance	
					Debit	Credit

P3-26A or P3-26B (continued)

Requirement 2

GENERAL JOURNAL   Page _____

Date	Accounts and Explanations	PR	Debit	Credit

3-20

Name _____

Section _____

P3-27A or P3-27B Adjusting Entries for Deferrals and Accruals

GENERAL JOURNAL

Page _____

Date	Accounts and Explanations	PR	Debit	Credit

P3-28A or P3-28B Preparation of Adjusting Entries and Financial Statements

Requirements 1 and 3

GENERAL LEDGER

_____ Acct. No. _____

Date	Explanation	PR	Debit	Credit	Balance	
					Debit	Credit

_____ Acct. No. _____

Date	Explanation	PR	Debit	Credit	Balance	
					Debit	Credit

_____ Acct. No. _____

Date	Explanation	PR	Debit	Credit	Balance	
					Debit	Credit

_____ Acct. No. _____

Date	Explanation	PR	Debit	Credit	Balance	
					Debit	Credit

P3-28A or P3-28B Requirements 1 and 3 (continued)

GENERAL LEDGER

Acct. No. _____

Date	Explanation	PR	Debit	Credit	Balance Debit	Credit

Acct. No. _____

Date	Explanation	PR	Debit	Credit	Balance Debit	Credit

Acct. No. _____

Date	Explanation	PR	Debit	Credit	Balance Debit	Credit

Acct. No. _____

Date	Explanation	PR	Debit	Credit	Balance Debit	Credit

Name _____

Section _____

P3-28A or P3-28B Requirements 1 and 3 (continued)

GENERAL LEDGER

_____ Acct. No. _____

Date	Explanation	PR	Debit	Credit	Balance	
					Debit	Credit

_____ Acct. No. _____

Date	Explanation	PR	Debit	Credit	Balance	
					Debit	Credit

_____ Acct. No. _____

Date	Explanation	PR	Debit	Credit	Balance	
					Debit	Credit

_____ Acct. No. _____

Date	Explanation	PR	Debit	Credit	Balance	
					Debit	Credit

P3-28A or P3-28B Requirements 1 and 3 (continued)

GENERAL LEDGER

_____ Acct. No. _____

Date	Explanation	PR	Debit	Credit	Balance	
					Debit	Credit

_____ Acct. No. _____

Date	Explanation	PR	Debit	Credit	Balance	
					Debit	Credit

_____ Acct. No. _____

Date	Explanation	PR	Debit	Credit	Balance	
					Debit	Credit

_____ Acct. No. _____

Date	Explanation	PR	Debit	Credit	Balance	
					Debit	Credit

P3-28A or P3-28B Requirements 1 and 3 (continued)

GENERAL LEDGER

_____   Acct. No. _____

Date	Explanation	PR	Debit	Credit	Balance	
					Debit	Credit

_____   Acct. No. _____

Date	Explanation	PR	Debit	Credit	Balance	
					Debit	Credit

_____   Acct. No. _____

Date	Explanation	PR	Debit	Credit	Balance	
					Debit	Credit

_____   Acct. No. _____

Date	Explanation	PR	Debit	Credit	Balance	
					Debit	Credit

P3-28A or P3-28B Requirements 1 and 3 (continued)
GENERAL LEDGER

_____   Acct. No. _____

Date	Explanation	PR	Debit	Credit	Balance	
					Debit	Credit

_____   Acct. No. _____

Date	Explanation	PR	Debit	Credit	Balance	
					Debit	Credit

_____   Acct. No. _____

Date	Explanation	PR	Debit	Credit	Balance	
					Debit	Credit

P3-28A or P3-28B (continued)

Requirement 2

GENERAL JOURNAL

Date	Accounts and Explanations	PR	Debit	Credit

P3-28A or P3-28B (continued)

Requirement 4

Adjusted Trial Balance

Acct. No.	Account Title	Debits	Credits

P3-28A or P3-28B (continued)

Requirement 5

Income Statement

Statement of Owner's Equity

P3-28A or P3-28B Requirement 5 (continued)

Balance Sheet

_____

_____

P3-29A or P3-29B Adjustments and Effects on Statements

Requirements 1, 2, and 3

Item	Adjusting Journal Entry December 31, 1993	Financial Statement Classification	Amount Reported on Financial Statement

P3-30A or P3-30B (Appendix) Adjustments for Transactions Initially Recorded in Income Statement Accounts

GENERAL JOURNAL

Page _____

Date	Accounts and Explanations	PR	Debit	Credit

P3-31A or P3-31B Evaluation and Restatement of Financial Statements to Conform to Accrual Basis of Accounting

Requirement 1

Income Statement

Statement of Owner's Equity

P3-31A or P3-31B Requirement 1 (continued)

_____

Balance Sheet

_____

P3-31A or P3-31B Requirement 1 (continued)

_____
_____
_____
_____
_____
_____
_____
_____
_____
_____
_____
_____
_____
_____
_____
_____
_____
_____
_____
_____
_____
_____
_____
_____
_____
_____
_____
_____
_____
_____
_____
_____
_____
_____
_____
_____
_____
_____
_____
_____
_____
_____
_____
_____
_____
_____
_____
_____

P3-31A or P3-31B (continued)

Requirement 2

_____
_____
_____
_____
_____
_____
_____
_____
_____
_____
_____
_____
_____
_____
_____
_____
_____
_____
_____
_____
_____
_____
_____
_____
_____
_____
_____
_____
_____
_____
_____
_____
_____
_____
_____
_____
_____
_____
_____
_____
_____
_____
_____
_____

PRACTICE CASE

End-of-Period Adjusting Entries

Requirement 1

GENERAL JOURNAL

Page _____

Date	Accounts and Explanations	PR	Debit	Credit

3-41

Name _____

Section _____

Practice Case (continued)

Requirement 2

	Total Assets 12/31/93	Total Liabilities 12/31/93	Total Owner's Equity 12/31/93	Total Revenues 1993	Total Expenses 1993
a.					
b.					
c.					
d.					
e.					
f.					

BUSINESS DECISION AND COMMUNICATION PROBLEM

Accounting for Postretirement Benefits by Borden, Inc.

3-43

ETHICAL DILEMMA

Extending Useful Life of Assets to Raise Net Income

_____
_____
_____
_____
_____
_____
_____
_____
_____
_____
_____
_____
_____
_____
_____
_____
_____
_____
_____
_____
_____
_____
_____
_____
_____
_____
_____
_____
_____
_____
_____
_____
_____
_____
_____
_____
_____
_____
_____
_____
_____
_____
_____
_____
_____
_____

Name _____

Section _____

CHAPTER 4
Completion of the Accounting Cycle

EXERCISES
E4-17 Partial Work Sheet

Account Title	Income Statement		Balance Sheet	
	Debit	Credit	Debit	Credit
Totals				

4-1

E4-18 Work Sheet Completion

THOI COMPANY
Work Sheet
For the Year Ended December 31, 1993

Account Title	Adjusted Trial Balance		Income Statement		Balance Sheet	
	Debit	Credit	Debit	Credit	Debit	Credit

E4-19 Work Sheet and Income Statement

[For E4-19 Requirements 1 and 2, see foldout section at back of book.]

Requirement 3

Income Statement

Name _____

Section _____

E4-20 Work Sheet with Adjustments and Discussion

[For E4-20 Requirements 1 and 2, see foldout section at back of book.]

Requirement 3

_____

_____

_____

_____

_____

_____

_____

_____

_____

_____

_____

Name _____

Section _____

E4-21 Adjusting, Closing, and Future-year Entries for Accruals

Requirement 1

GENERAL JOURNAL

Page _____

Date	Accounts and Explanations	PR	Debit	Credit

4-5

E4-21 (continued)

Requirement 2

GENERAL JOURNAL

Page _____

Date	Accounts and Explanations	PR	Debit	Credit

E4-22 Adjusting Entries and Their Statement Effect

GENERAL JOURNAL

Page _____

Date	Accounts and Explanations	PR	Debit	Credit

(continued)

E4-22 (continued)

Date		Accounts and Explanations	PR	Debit	Credit

E4-23 Closing Entries

GENERAL JOURNAL

_____ Page _____

Date	Accounts and Explanations	PR	Debit	Credit

E4-24 Closing Entries

Requirement 1

GENERAL JOURNAL

_____

Date	Accounts and Explanations	PR	Debit	Credit

E4-24 (continued)

Requirement 2

Postclosing Trial Balance

Acct. No.	Account Title	Debits	Credits

E4-25 Effect of Errors in Adjustments on Statements

Requirement 1

GENERAL JOURNAL   Page _____

Date	Accounts and Explanations	PR	Debit	Credit

E4-25 (continued)

Requirement 2

Income Statement

Statement of Owner's Equity

E4-25 Requirement 2 (continued)

_____

Balance Sheet

_____

E4-26 Reversing Entries (Appendix 4A)

GENERAL JOURNAL

Date	Accounts and Explanations	PR	Debit	Credit

E4-27 Journal Entries for a Corporation (Appendix 4B)

GENERAL JOURNAL

Date	Accounts and Explanations	PR	Debit	Credit

E4-28 Financial Statements for a Corporation (Appendix 4B)

Income Statement

Statement of Retained Earnings

E4-28 (continued)

_____

Balance Sheet

_____

A AND B PROBLEMS

P4-29A or P4-29B Work Sheet and End-of-Period Statements (No Adjustments)

Requirements 1 and 2

(continued)

Work Sheet

Account Title	Adjusted Trial Balance		Income Statement		Balance Sheet	
	Debit	Credit	Debit	Credit	Debit	Credit

4-19

P4-29A or P4-29B Requirements 1 and 2 (continued)

Account Title	Debit	Credit	Debit	Credit	Debit	Credit

P4-29A or P4-29B (continued)

Requirement 3

Income Statement

Statement of Owner's Equity

Name _____

Section _____

P4-29A or P4-29B Requirement 3 (continued)

_____

Balance Sheet

_____

(continued)

4-22

P4-29A or P4-29B   Requirement 3 (continued)

P4-30A or P4-30B Completion of a Work Sheet

[For P4-30A or P4-30B Requirements 1 and 2, see foldout section at back of book.]

Requirement 3

_____
_____
_____
_____
_____
_____
_____
_____
_____
_____
_____
_____
_____
_____
_____
_____
_____
_____
_____
_____
_____
_____
_____

P4-31A or P4-31B The Complete Accounting Cycle

[For P4-31A or P4-31B Requirements 3 and 4, see foldout section at back of book.]

Requirements 1, 2, 6, and 7

GENERAL LEDGER
Cash   Acct. No. __101__

Date	Explanation	PR	Debit	Credit	Balance Debit	Balance Credit

_____   Acct. No. _____

Date	Explanation	PR	Debit	Credit	Balance Debit	Balance Credit

_____   Acct. No. _____

Date	Explanation	PR	Debit	Credit	Balance Debit	Balance Credit

P4-31A or P4-31B Requirements 1, 2, 6, and 7 (continued)

_____ Acct. _____

Date	Explanation	PR	Debit	Credit	Balance Debit	Balance Credit

_____ Acct. _____

Date	Explanation	PR	Debit	Credit	Balance Debit	Balance Credit

_____ Acct. _____

Date	Explanation	PR	Debit	Credit	Balance Debit	Balance Credit

_____ Acct. _____

Date	Explanation	PR	Debit	Credit	Balance Debit	Balance Credit

P4-31A or P4-31B Requirements 1, 2, 6, and 7 (continued)

_____ Acct. No. _____

Date	Explanation	PR	Debit	Credit	Balance	
					Debit	Credit

_____ Acct. No. _____

Date	Explanation	PR	Debit	Credit	Balance	
					Debit	Credit

_____ Acct. No. _____

Date	Explanation	PR	Debit	Credit	Balance	
					Debit	Credit

_____ Acct. No. _____

Date	Explanation	PR	Debit	Credit	Balance	
					Debit	Credit

P4-31A or P4-31B Requirements 1, 2, 6, and 7 (continued)

_____ Acct. No. _____

Date	Explanation	PR	Debit	Credit	Balance Debit	Balance Credit

_____ Acct. No. _____

Date	Explanation	PR	Debit	Credit	Balance Debit	Balance Credit

_____ Acct. No. _____

Date	Explanation	PR	Debit	Credit	Balance Debit	Balance Credit

_____ Acct. No. _____

Date	Explanation	PR	Debit	Credit	Balance Debit	Balance Credit

P4-31A or P4-31B Requirements 1, 2, 6, and 7 (continued)

_____ Acct. No. _____

Date	Explanation	PR	Debit	Credit	Balance	
					Debit	Credit

_____ Acct. No. _____

Date	Explanation	PR	Debit	Credit	Balance	
					Debit	Credit

_____ Acct. No. _____

Date	Explanation	PR	Debit	Credit	Balance	
					Debit	Credit

P4-31A or P4-31B Requirement 2 (continued)

GENERAL JOURNAL

Page _____

Date	Accounts and Explanations	PR	Debit	Credit

(continued)

P4-31A or P4-31B Requirement 2 (continued)

Date	Accounts and Explanations	PR	Debit	Credit

P4-31A or P4-31B (continued)

[For P4-31A or P4-31B Requirements 3 and 4, see foldout section at back of book.]

Requirement 4

Income Statement

<table>
<tr><td></td><td></td><td></td><td></td><td></td><td></td><td></td></tr>
<tr><td></td><td></td><td></td><td></td><td></td><td></td><td></td></tr>
</table>

Statement of Owner's Equity

<table>
<tr><td></td><td></td><td></td><td></td><td></td><td></td><td></td></tr>
<tr><td></td><td></td><td></td><td></td><td></td><td></td><td></td></tr>
</table>

P4-31A or P4-31B Requirement 4 (continued)

_____

Balance Sheet

_____

P4-31A or P4-31B (continued)

Requirement 5

GENERAL JOURNAL
Adjusting Entries

Page _____

Date	Accounts and Explanations	PR	Debit	Credit

P4-31A or P4-31B (continued)

Requirement 7

GENERAL JOURNAL
Closing Entries

Page _____

Date	Accounts and Explanations	PR	Debit	Credit

P4-31A or P4-31B (continued)

Requirement 8

<u>Postclosing Trial Balance</u>

Acct. No.	Account Title	Debits	Credits

P4-32A or P4-32B Closing Entries and Postclosing Trial Balance

Requirement 1

GENERAL LEDGER

_____ Acct. No. _____

Date	Explanation	PR	Debit	Credit	Balance Debit	Credit

_____ Acct. No. _____

Date	Explanation	PR	Debit	Credit	Balance Debit	Credit

_____ Acct. No. _____

Date	Explanation	PR	Debit	Credit	Balance Debit	Credit

P4-32A or P4-32B Requirement 1 (continued)

_____ Acct. No. _____

Date	Explanation	PR	Debit	Credit	Balance	
					Debit	Credit

_____ Acct. No. _____

Date	Explanation	PR	Debit	Credit	Balance	
					Debit	Credit

_____ Acct. No. _____

Date	Explanation	PR	Debit	Credit	Balance	
					Debit	Credit

_____ Acct. No. _____

Date	Explanation	PR	Debit	Credit	Balance	
					Debit	Credit

P4-32A or P4-32B Requirement 1 (continued)

_____   Acct. No. _____

Date	Explanation	PR	Debit	Credit	Balance	
					Debit	**Credit**

_____   Acct. No. _____

Date	Explanation	PR	Debit	Credit	Balance	
					Debit	**Credit**

P4-32A or P4-32B (continued)

Requirement 2

GENERAL JOURNAL
Closing Entries

Page _____

Date	Accounts and Explanations	PR	Debit	Credit

P4-32A or P4-32B (continued)

Requirement 3

Postclosing Trial Balance

Acct. No.	Account Title	Debits	Credits

P4-33A The Issue of Proprietor Salary or

P4-33B Financial Statements and Interpretation of Adjustment

Requirement 1

Income Statement

Requirement 2

Statement of Owner's Equity

P4-33A (continued)

Requirement 3

_____
_____
_____
_____
_____
_____
_____
_____
_____
_____
_____
_____
_____
_____
_____
_____
_____
_____
_____
_____
_____

Name _____

Section _____

P4-34A or P4-34B Adjustment Methods and Reversing Entries
(includes Appendixes 3A and 4A Requirement)

Requirements 1, 2, 4, and 5

GENERAL LEDGER

Acct. No. _____

Date	Explanation	PR	Debit	Credit	Balance	
					Debit	Credit

Acct. No. _____

Date	Explanation	PR	Debit	Credit	Balance	
					Debit	Credit

Acct. No. _____

Date	Explanation	PR	Debit	Credit	Balance	
					Debit	Credit

4-45

P4-34A or P4-34B Requirements 1, 2, 4, and 5 (continued)

Acct. No. _____

Date	Explanation	PR	Debit	Credit	Balance	
					Debit	Credit

Acct. No. _____

Date	Explanation	PR	Debit	Credit	Balance	
					Debit	Credit

Acct. No. _____

Date	Explanation	PR	Debit	Credit	Balance	
					Debit	Credit

P4-34A or P4-34B Requirements 1, 2, 4, and 5 (continued)

_____ Acct. No. _____

Date	Explanation	PR	Debit	Credit	Balance Debit	Balance Credit

_____ Acct. No. _____

Date	Explanation	PR	Debit	Credit	Balance Debit	Balance Credit

_____ Acct. No. _____

Date	Explanation	PR	Debit	Credit	Balance Debit	Balance Credit

P4-34A or P4-34B Requirements 1, 2, 4, and 5 (continued)

Acct. No. _____

Date	Explanation	PR	Debit	Credit	Balance Debit	Credit

Acct. No. _____

Date	Explanation	PR	Debit	Credit	Balance Debit	Credit

Acct. No. _____

Date	Explanation	PR	Debit	Credit	Balance Debit	Credit

P4-34A or P4-34B Requirements 1, 2, 4, and 5 (continued)

_____   Acct. No. _____

Date	Explanation	PR	Debit	Credit	Balance Debit	Balance Credit

P4-34A or P4-34B (continued)

Requirement 2

GENERAL JOURNAL
Adjusting Entries

Date	Accounts and Explanations	PR	Debit	Credit

P4-34A or P4-34B (continued)

Requirement 3

GENERAL JOURNAL
Closing Entries

Date	Accounts and Explanations	PR	Debit	Credit

Name _____

Section _____

P4-34A or P4-34B (continued)

Requirement 5

GENERAL JOURNAL
Reversing Entries

Page _____

Date	Accounts and Explanations	PR	Debit	Credit

P4-35A or P4-35B End-of-Period Process for a Corporation (Appendix 4B)

[For P4-35A or P4-35B Requirements 1 and 2, see foldout section at back of book.]

Requirement 3

_____

Income Statement

_____

4-53

Name _____

Section _____

P4-35A or P4-35B Requirement 3 (continued)

Statement of Retained Earnings

Balance Sheet

(continued)

P4-35A or P4-35B Requirement 3 (continued)

PRACTICE CASE

Completion of the Accounting Cycle

[For Practice Case Requirement 1, see foldout section at back of book.]

Requirement 2

Income Statement

Statement of Owner's Equity

Practice Case Requirement 2 (continued)

_____

Balance Sheet

_____

Practice Case (continued)

Requirement 3

GENERAL JOURNAL
Adjusting Entries

Page _____

Date	Accounts and Explanations	PR	Debit	Credit

Practice Case (continued)

Requirement 4

GENERAL JOURNAL
Closing Entries

Date	Accounts and Explanations	PR	Debit	Credit

Name _____

Section _____

BUSINESS DECISION AND COMMUNICATION PROBLEM

Analysis of AT&T

_____

_____

_____

_____

_____

_____

_____

_____

_____

_____

_____

_____

_____

_____

_____

_____

_____

_____

_____

_____

_____

_____

_____

_____

_____

_____

_____

_____

_____

_____

_____

_____

_____

_____

_____

_____

_____

_____

_____

_____

4-61

ETHICAL DILEMMA

Changing the Company's Accounting Methods to Raise Net Income

Name _____

Section _____

MINI PRACTICE SET I

Requirements 1, 3, 6, and 7 (when assigned after Chapter 4)

Requirements 1, 3, and 5 (when assigned after Chapter 3)

GENERAL LEDGER
Cash

Acct. No. __101__

Date	Explanation	PR	Debit	Credit	Balance Debit	Balance Credit

4-65

Mini Practice Set (continued)

Requirements 1, 3, 6, and 7 (when assigned after Chapter 4)

Requirements 1, 3, and 5 (when assigned after Chapter 3)

Accounts Receivable

Acct. No. __111__

Date	Explanation	PR	Debit	Credit	Balance	
					Debit	Credit

Supplies

Acct. No. __137__

Date	Explanation	PR	Debit	Credit	Balance	
					Debit	Credit

Prepaid Insurance

Acct. No. __141__

Date	Explanation	PR	Debit	Credit	Balance	
					Debit	Credit

Mini Practice Set (continued)

Requirements 1, 3, 6, and 7 (when assigned after Chapter 4)

Requirements 1, 3, and 5 (when assigned after Chapter 3)

Equipment
Acct. No. __159__

Date	Explanation	PR	Debit	Credit	Balance Debit	Balance Credit

Accumulated Depreciation – Equipment
Acct. No. __160__

Date	Explanation	PR	Debit	Credit	Balance Debit	Balance Credit

Trucks
Acct. No. __169__

Date	Explanation	PR	Debit	Credit	Balance Debit	Balance Credit

Accumulated Depreciation – Trucks
Acct. No. __170__

Date	Explanation	PR	Debit	Credit	Balance Debit	Balance Credit

Name _____

Section _____

Mini Practice Set (continued)

Requirements 1, 3, 6, and 7 (when assigned after Chapter 4)

Requirements 1, 3, and 5 (when assigned after Chapter 3)

Accounts Payable
Acct. No. __201__

Date	Explanation	PR	Debit	Credit	Balance	
					Debit	Credit

Notes Payable
Acct. No. __202__

Date	Explanation	PR	Debit	Credit	Balance	
					Debit	Credit

Interest Payable
Acct. No. __204__

Date	Explanation	PR	Debit	Credit	Balance	
					Debit	Credit

Mini Practice Set (continued)

Requirements 1, 3, 6, and 7 (when assigned after Chapter 4)

Requirements 1, 3, and 5 (when assigned after Chapter 3)

Wages Payable

Acct. No. __205__

Date	Explanation	PR	Debit	Credit	Balance Debit	Balance Credit

Unearned Service Revenue

Acct. No. __233__

Date	Explanation	PR	Debit	Credit	Balance Debit	Balance Credit

B. Frank, Capital

Acct. No. __301__

Date	Explanation	PR	Debit	Credit	Balance Debit	Balance Credit

Mini Practice Set (continued)

Requirements 1, 3, 6, and 7 (when assigned after Chapter 4)

Requirements 1, 3, and 5 (when assigned after Chapter 3)

B. Frank, Withdrawals

Acct. No. __311__

Date	Explanation	PR	Debit	Credit	Balance Debit	Balance Credit

Service Revenue

Acct. No. __413__

Date	Explanation	PR	Debit	Credit	Balance Debit	Balance Credit

Advertising Expense

Acct. No. __616__

Date	Explanation	PR	Debit	Credit	Balance Debit	Balance Credit

Mini Practice Set (continued)

Requirements 1, 3, 6, and 7 (when assigned after Chapter 4)

Requirements 1, 3, and 5 (when assigned after Chapter 3)

Wages Expense

Acct. No. __705__

Date	Explanation	PR	Debit	Credit	Balance Debit	Balance Credit

Rent Expense – Building

Acct. No. __711__

Date	Explanation	PR	Debit	Credit	Balance Debit	Balance Credit

Supplies Expense

Acct. No. __718__

Date	Explanation	PR	Debit	Credit	Balance Debit	Balance Credit

Mini Practice Set (continued)

Requirements 1, 3, 6, and 7 (when assigned after Chapter 4)

Requirements 1, 3, and 5 (when assigned after Chapter 3)

Insurance Expense

Acct. No. __719__

Date	Explanation	PR	Debit	Credit	Balance Debit	Balance Credit

Utilities Expense

Acct. No. __721__

Date	Explanation	PR	Debit	Credit	Balance Debit	Balance Credit

Communication Expense

Acct. No. __722__

Date	Explanation	PR	Debit	Credit	Balance Debit	Balance Credit

Repairs Expense

Acct. No. __723__

Date	Explanation	PR	Debit	Credit	Balance Debit	Balance Credit

Mini Practice Set (continued)

Requirements 1, 3, 6, and 7 (when assigned after Chapter 4)

Requirements 1, 3, and 5 (when assigned after Chapter 3)

Gas and Oil Expense

Acct. No. __726__

Date	Explanation	PR	Debit	Credit	Balance Debit	Balance Credit

Depreciation Expense — Equipment

Acct. No. __753__

Date	Explanation	PR	Debit	Credit	Balance Debit	Balance Credit

Depreciation Expense — Trucks

Acct. No. __759__

Date	Explanation	PR	Debit	Credit	Balance Debit	Balance Credit

Interest Expense

Acct. No. __852__

Date	Explanation	PR	Debit	Credit	Balance Debit	Balance Credit

Mini Practice Set (continued)

Requirements 1, 3, 6, and 7 (when assigned after Chapter 4)

Requirements 1, 3, and 5 (when assigned after Chapter 3)

Income Summary   Acct. No. __999__

Date	Explanation	PR	Debit	Credit	Balance Debit	Balance Credit

Mini Practice Set (continued)

Requirement 2

GENERAL JOURNAL

Date	Accounts and Explanations	PR	Debit	Credit

(continued)

4-75

Mini Practice Set Requirement 2 (continued)

GENERAL JOURNAL

Date	Accounts and Explanations	PR	Debit	Credit

(continued)

Name _____

Section _____

Mini Practice Set Requirement 2 (continued)

GENERAL JOURNAL

Page _____

Date	Accounts and Explanations	PR	Debit	Credit

(continued)

Mini Practice Set Requirement 2 (continued)

GENERAL JOURNAL

Page _____

Date	Accounts and Explanations	PR	Debit	Credit

Mini Practice Set (continued)

[For Requirement 4 (when assigned after Chapter 4), see foldout section at back of book.]

Requirement 4 (when assigned after Chapter 3)

Unadjusted Trial Balance

Acct. No.	Account Title	Debits	Credits

Mini Practice Set (continued)

Requirement 5 (when assigned after Chapter 3)

Requirement 6 (when assigned after Chapter 4)

GENERAL JOURNAL

_____ Page _____

Date	Accounts and Explanations	PR	Debit	Credit

Mini Practice Set (continued)

Requirement 6 (when assigned after Chapter 3)

Adjusted Trial Balance

Acct. No.	Account Title	Debits	Credits

Name _____

Section _____

Mini Practice Set (continued)

Requirement 5 (when assigned after Chapter 4)

Requirement 7 (when assigned after Chapter 3)

Income Statement

4-82

Mini Practice Set (continued)

Requirement 5 (when assigned after Chapter 4)

Requirement 7 (when asigned after Chapter 3)

Statement of Owner's Equity

Mini Practice Set (continued)

Requirement 5 (when assigned after Chapter 4)

Requirement 7 (when assigned after Chapter 3)

_____

Balance Sheet

_____

Mini Practice Set (continued)

Requirement 7 (when assigned after Chapter 4)

GENERAL JOURNAL
Closing Entries

Page _____

Date	Accounts and Explanations	PR	Debit	Credit

4-85

Mini Practice Set (continued)

Requirement 8 (when assigned after Chapter 4)

_____

Postclosing Trial Balance

_____

Acct. No.	Account Title	Debits	Credits

4-86

CHAPTER 5
Accounting for a Merchandising Business

EXERCISES
E5-16 Journalizing Sales Transactions

GENERAL JOURNAL

Page _____

Date	Accounts and Explanations	PR	Debit	Credit

E5-17 Journalizing Purchases Transactions

GENERAL JOURNAL

Date	Accounts and Explanations	PR	Debit	Credit

(continued)

E5-17 (continued)

Date	Accounts and Explanations	PR	Debit	Credit

E5-18 Trade Discounts

GENERAL JOURNAL

Page _____

Date	Accounts and Explanations	PR	Debit	Credit

E5-19 Sales Discounts: Partial Payment

GENERAL JOURNAL

Page _____

Date	Accounts and Explanations	PR	Debit	Credit

E5-20 Calculation of Total Cost of Goods Available and Cost of Goods Sold

_____

_____

_____

_____

_____

_____

_____

_____

_____

_____

_____

E5-21 Computation of Net Sales, Net Purchases, Cost of Goods Sold, and Gross Margin on Sales

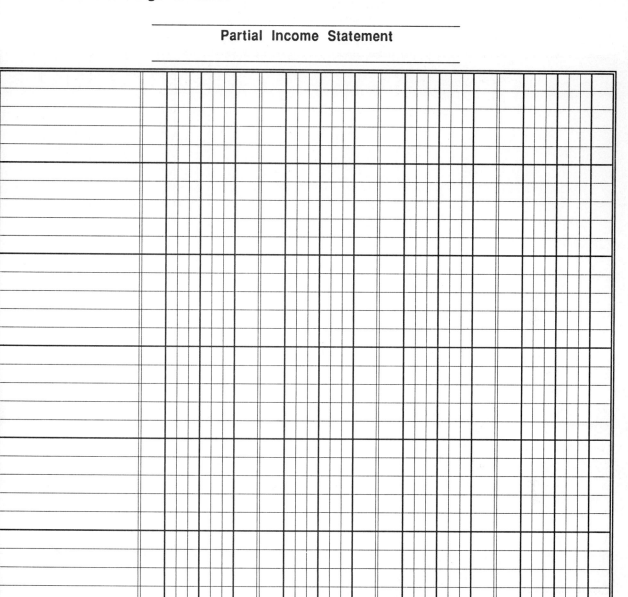

Partial Income Statement

E5-22 Calculation of Gross Sales

_____

Income Statement

_____

Computations:

_____
_____
_____
_____
_____

E5-23 Inventories in the Work Sheet (Instructor to choose approach)

[For E5-23, see foldout section at back of book.]

E5-24 Determination of Missing Income Statement Amounts

Kona Company

_____
_____
_____
_____
_____
_____
_____
_____
_____
_____
_____
_____
_____
_____
_____
_____
_____
_____
_____
_____
_____
_____
_____
_____
_____
_____
_____
_____
_____
_____
_____
_____

E5-24 (continued)

Oahu Company

E5-24 (continued)

Hilo Company

_____

_____

_____

_____

_____

_____

_____

_____

_____

_____

_____

_____

_____

_____

_____

_____

_____

_____

_____

_____

_____

_____

_____

_____

_____

_____

_____

_____

_____

_____

_____

E5-25 Multiple-Step Income Statement

Income Statement

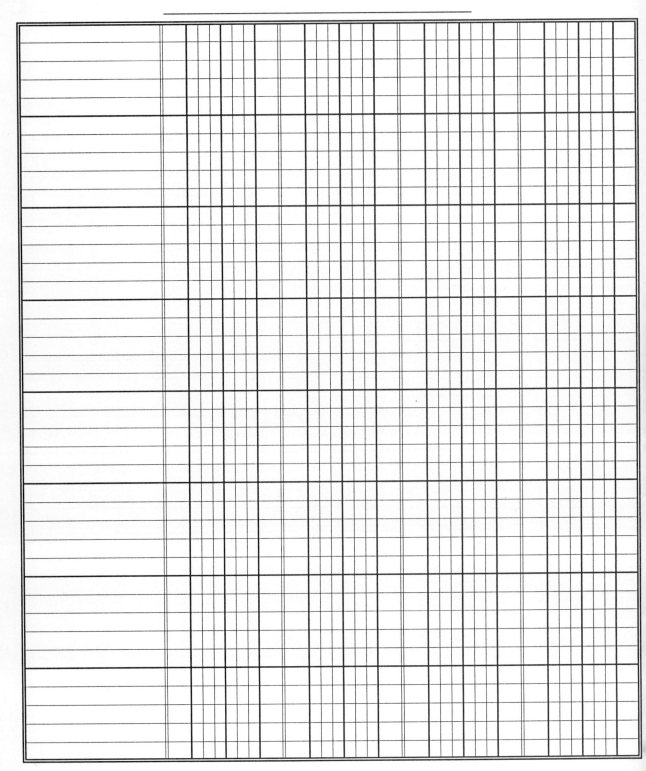

Name _____

Section _____

E5-26 Closing Entries

GENERAL JOURNAL

Page _____

Date	Accounts and Explanations	PR	Debit	Credit

E5-27 Recordkeeping of Purchases: Net Price Method

Requirement 1

GENERAL JOURNAL

Page _____

Date	Accounts and Explanations	PR	Debit	Credit

Requirement 2

_____

_____

_____

_____

_____

_____

_____

_____

_____

_____

_____

_____

_____

_____

_____

_____

_____

_____

_____

_____

_____

_____

_____

_____

(continued)

E5-27

Requirement 2 (continued)

_____
_____
_____
_____
_____

Requirement 3

_____
_____
_____
_____
_____
_____
_____
_____
_____
_____
_____
_____
_____
_____
_____
_____
_____
_____
_____
_____
_____
_____
_____

A AND B PROBLEMS

P5-28A or P5-28B Use of Merchandising Accounts

GENERAL JOURNAL

Page _____

Date	Accounts and Explanations	PR	Debit	Credit

(continued)

P5-28A or P5-28B (continued)

Date	Accounts and Explanations	PR	Debit	Credit

5-16

P5-29A Partial Income Statement

Partial Income Statement

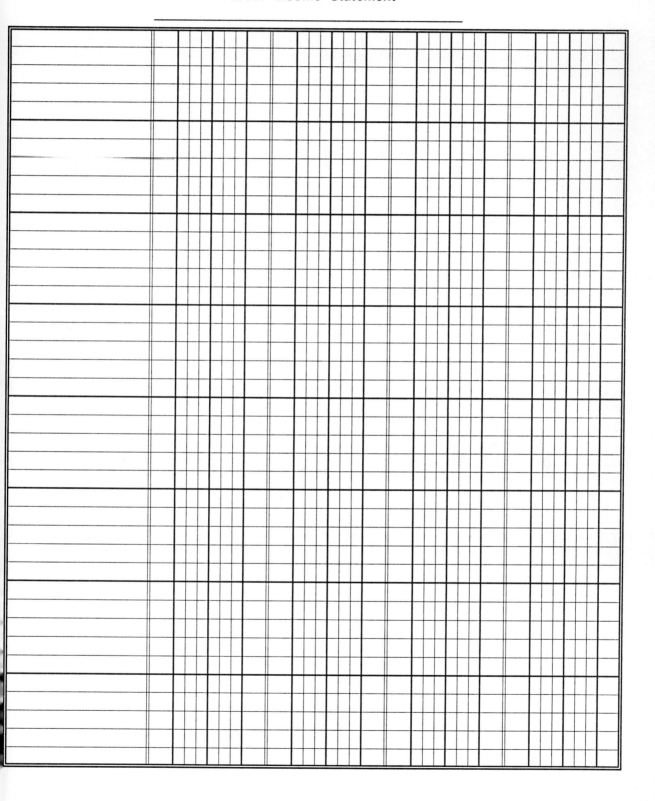

Name _____

Section _____

P5-29B Cost of Goods Sold Schedule

_____

_____

_____

P5-30A or P5-30B Income Statement and Closing Entries

Requirement 1

<u>_____</u>

Income Statement

<u>_____</u>

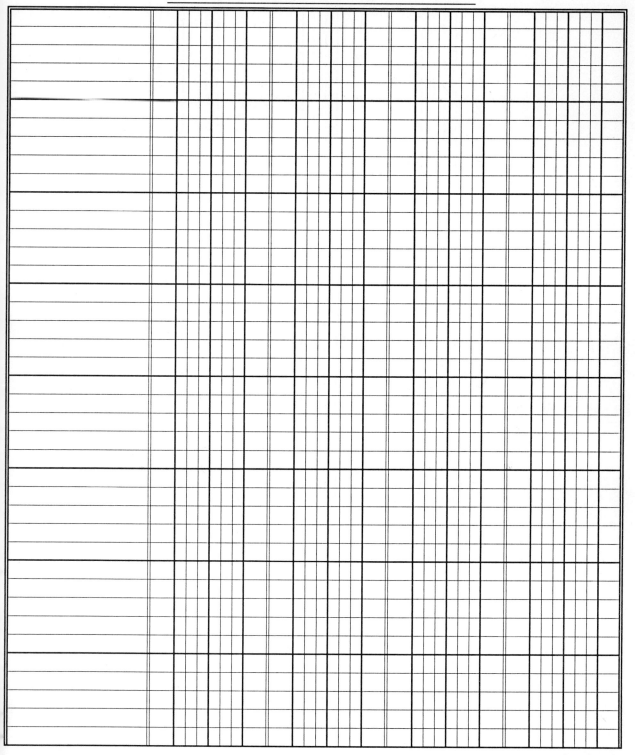

(continued)

Name _____

Section _____

P5-30A or P5-30B Requirement 1 (continued)

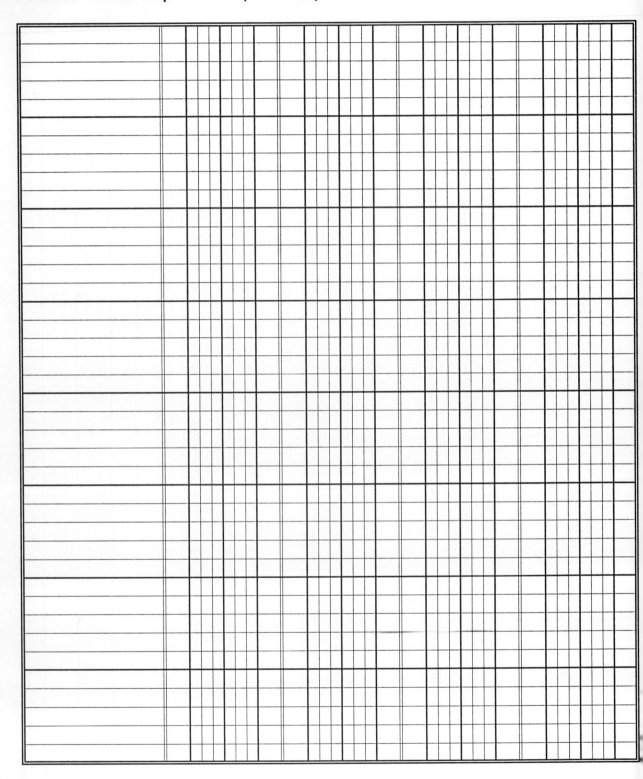

P5-30A or P5-30B (continued)

Requirement 2

GENERAL JOURNAL

Date	Accounts and Explanations	PR	Debit	Credit

P5-31A or P5-31B Journalizing Transactions for a Retail Store

Requirement 1

GENERAL JOURNAL

Page _____

Date	Accounts and Explanations	PR	Debit	Credit

(continued)

P5-31A or P5-31B Requirement 1 (continued)

Date	Accounts and Explanations	PR	Debit	Credit

P5-31A or P5-31B (continued)

Requirement 2

GENERAL LEDGER
Cash   Acct. No. __101__

Date	Explanation	PR	Debit	Credit	Balance	
					Debit	Credit

Accounts Receivable   Acct. No. __111__

Date	Explanation	PR	Debit	Credit	Balance	
					Debit	Credit

P5-31A or P5-31B Requirement 2 (continued)

Accounts Payable

Acct. No. **201**

Date	Explanation	PR	Debit	Credit	Balance Debit	Balance Credit

Sales

Acct. No. **401**

Date	Explanation	PR	Debit	Credit	Balance Debit	Balance Credit

Sales Returns and Allowances

Acct. No. **402**

Date	Explanation	PR	Debit	Credit	Balance Debit	Balance Credit

P5-31A or P5-31B Requirement 2 (continued)

Sales Discounts

Date	Explanation	PR	Debit	Credit	Balance Debit	Balance Credit

Purchases

Date	Explanation	PR	Debit	Credit	Balance Debit	Balance Credit

Transportation In

Date	Explanation	PR	Debit	Credit	Balance Debit	Balance Credit

Purchases Returns and Allowances

Date	Explanation	PR	Debit	Credit	Balance Debit	Balance Credit

P5-31A or P5-31B Requirement 2 (continued)

Purchases Discounts

Acct. No. __504__

Date	Explanation	PR	Debit	Credit	Balance Debit	Balance Credit

Sales Wages Expense

Acct. No. __602__

Date	Explanation	PR	Debit	Credit	Balance Debit	Balance Credit

Advertising Expense

Acct. No. __616__

Date	Explanation	PR	Debit	Credit	Balance Debit	Balance Credit

Delivery Expense

Acct. No. __621__

Date	Explanation	PR	Debit	Credit	Balance Debit	Balance Credit

P5-31A or P5-31B Requirement 2 (continued)

Utilities Expense

Acct. No. __625__

Date	Explanation	PR	Debit	Credit	Balance	
					Debit	Credit

Office Wages Expense

Acct. No. __703__

Date	Explanation	PR	Debit	Credit	Balance	
					Debit	Credit

P5-31A or P5-31B (continued)

Requirement 3

<u>_____</u>
Income Statement
<u>_____</u>

P5-32A or P5-32B Completion of a Worksheet, Preparation of Statements, Adjusting and Closing Entries

[For P5-32A or P5-32B, Requirement 1, see foldout section at back of book.]

Requirement 2

Income Statement

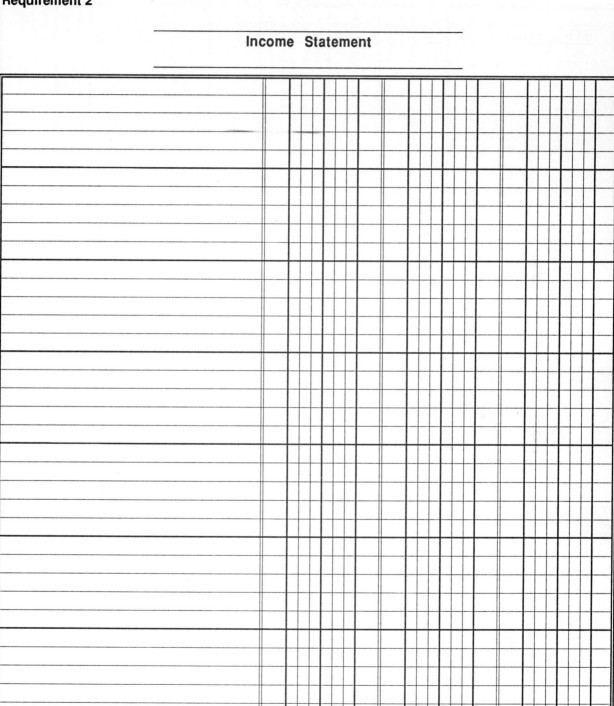

P5-32A or P5-32B Requirement 2 (continued)

Statement of Owner's Equity

P5-32A or P5-32B Requirement 2 (continued)

_____

Balance Sheet

_____

P5-32A or P5-32B (continued)

Requirement 3

GENERAL JOURNAL

Date	Accounts and Explanations	PR	Debit	Credit

(continued)

P5-32A or P5-32B Requirement 3 [closing approach] (continued)

Date	Accounts and Explanations	PR	Debit	Credit

P5-33A or P5-33B Recording Purchases Net of Discount

Requirement 1a

GENERAL JOURNAL

Date	Accounts and Explanations	PR	Debit	Credit

P5-33A or P5-33B (continued)

Requirement 1b

Partial Income Statement

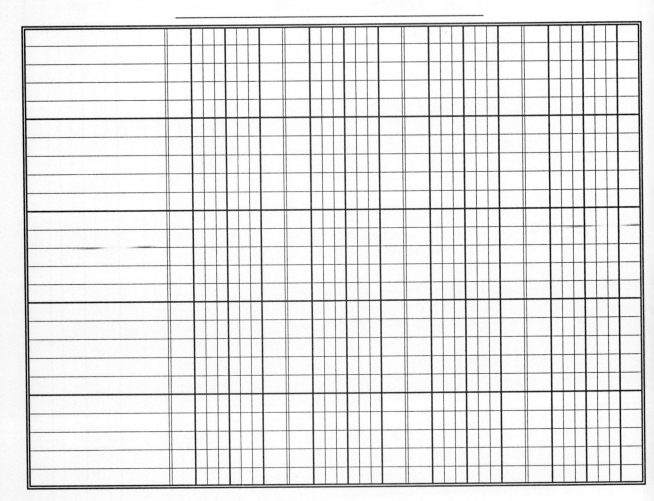

P5-33A or P5-33B (continued)

Requirement 2a

GENERAL JOURNAL

Date	Accounts and Explanations	PR	Debit	Credit

P5-33A or P5-33B (continued)

Requirement 2b

Partial Income Statement

Date	Accounts and Explanations	PR	Debit	Credit

Requirement 3

_____

_____

_____

_____

_____

_____

P5-34A Comparison of Gross Margins and Net Operating Margins for Toys "R" Us, Inc., or

P5-34B Comparison of Gross Margins and Net Operating Margins for J. C. Penney, Inc.

Requirement 1

Requirement 2

P5-34A or P5-34B (continued)

Requirement 3

_____
_____
_____
_____
_____
_____
_____
_____
_____
_____
_____
_____
_____
_____
_____
_____
_____
_____
_____
_____
_____
_____
_____
_____
_____

Requirement 4

_____
_____
_____
_____
_____
_____
_____
_____
_____
_____
_____
_____
_____
_____

Name _____

Section _____

PRACTICE CASE

Preparing a Multiple-step Income Statement, Statement of Owner's Equity, and Balance Sheet and Journalizing Closing Entries for a Merchandising Business

Requirement 1

_____

Income Statement

_____

Practice Case (continued)

Requirement 2

Statement of Owner's Equity

Practice Case (continued)

Requirement 3

Balance Sheet

Practice Case (continued)

Requirement 4

GENERAL JOURNAL

_____ Page _____

Date	Accounts and Explanations	PR	Debit	Credit

BUSINESS DECISION AND COMMUNICATION PROBLEM

Improving Profitability

_____

ETHICAL DILEMMA

Predating Sales Transactions

CHAPTER 6
Special Journals and Accounting Systems

EXERCISES

E6-18 Identification of Journal to Be Used

_____
_____
_____
_____
_____
_____
_____
_____
_____
_____
_____
_____
_____
_____
_____
_____
_____
_____
_____
_____
_____
_____
_____
_____

E6-19 Use of Sales Journal

SALES JOURNAL

Date		Account Debited	Terms	PR	Amount

E6-20   Use of Cash Receipts Journal

CASH RECEIPTS JOURNAL   Page _____

Date	Account Debited/Credited	PR	Debits			Credits		
			Cash	Sales Disc.	Other Accounts	Accounts Receivable	Sales	Other Accounts

E6–21   Use of Purchases Journal

PURCHASES JOURNAL   Page _____

Date	Account Credited	Terms	PR	Credit	Debits	
				Accounts Payable	Purchases	Office Supplies

E6-22 Use of Cash Payments Journal

CASH PAYMENTS JOURNAL

Date	Ck. No.	Account Debited/Credited	PR	Credits			Debits		
				Cash	Purch. Disc.	Other Accounts	Accounts Payable	Purchases	Other Accounts

E6-23 Posting from Sales Journal

GENERAL LEDGER
Accounts Receivable

Acct. No. __111__

Date	Explanation	PR	Debit	Credit	Balance Debit	Balance Credit

Sales

Acct. No. __401__

Date	Explanation	PR	Debit	Credit	Balance Debit	Balance Credit

ACCOUNTS RECEIVABLE SUBSIDIARY LEDGER
Eau Claire Supply

Acct. No. __4__

Date	Explanation	PR	Debit	Credit	Balance Debit	Balance Credit

Hampshire's, Inc.

Acct. No. __9__

Date	Explanation	PR	Debit	Credit	Balance Debit	Balance Credit

E6-23 (continued)

La Cross Company

Date	Explanation	PR	Debit	Credit	Balance Debit	Balance Credit

Oshkosh Stores, Inc.

Date	Explanation	PR	Debit	Credit	Balance Debit	Balance Credit

Whitewater Company

Date	Explanation	PR	Debit	Credit	Balance Debit	Balance Credit

E6-24 Posting from a Cash Receipts Journal

GENERAL LEDGER
Cash
Acct. No. __101__

Date	Explanation	PR	Debit	Credit	Balance Debit	Balance Credit

Accounts Receivable
Acct. No. __111__

Date	Explanation	PR	Debit	Credit	Balance Debit	Balance Credit

Notes Receivable
Acct. No. __115__

Date	Explanation	PR	Debit	Credit	Balance Debit	Balance Credit

Notes Payable
Acct. No. __202__

Date	Explanation	PR	Debit	Credit	Balance Debit	Balance Credit

E6-24 (continued)

W. Ray, Capital
Acct. No. __301__

Date	Explanation	PR	Debit	Credit	Balance Debit	Balance Credit

Sales
Acct. No. __401__

Date	Explanation	PR	Debit	Credit	Balance Debit	Balance Credit

Sales Discounts
Acct. No. __403__

Date	Explanation	PR	Debit	Credit	Balance Debit	Balance Credit

E6-24 (continued)

ACCOUNTS RECEIVABLE SUBSIDIARY LEDGER
Ella Gray

Acct. No. ___5___

Date	Explanation	PR	Debit	Credit	Balance	
					Debit	Credit

Arthur Jang

Acct. No. ___9___

Date	Explanation	PR	Debit	Credit	Balance	
					Debit	Credit

William Ramey

Acct. No. ___12___

Date	Explanation	PR	Debit	Credit	Balance	
					Debit	Credit

Name _____

Section _____

E6-25 Posting from Purchases Journal

GENERAL LEDGER
Store Supplies
Acct. No. __136__

Date	Explanation	PR	Debit	Credit	Balance Debit	Balance Credit

Accounts Payable
Acct. No. __201__

Date	Explanation	PR	Debit	Credit	Balance Debit	Balance Credit

Purchases
Acct. No. __501__

Date	Explanation	PR	Debit	Credit	Balance Debit	Balance Credit

ACCOUNTS PAYABLE SUBSIDIARY LEDGER
Andrea Erickson
Acct. No. __4__

Date	Explanation	PR	Debit	Credit	Balance Debit	Balance Credit

E6-25 (continued)

Bill Ford
Acct. No. ___8___

Date	Explanation	PR	Debit	Credit	Balance Debit	Balance Credit

Ed Henry
Acct. No. ___12___

Date	Explanation	PR	Debit	Credit	Balance Debit	Balance Credit

Ryan James
Acct. No. ___18___

Date	Explanation	PR	Debit	Credit	Balance Debit	Balance Credit

Gwen Owens
Acct. No. ___24___

Date	Explanation	PR	Debit	Credit	Balance Debit	Balance Credit

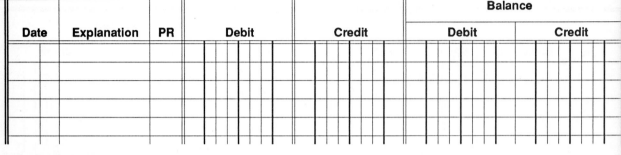

E6-26 Posting from Cash Payments Journal

GENERAL LEDGER
Cash

Acct. No. __101__

Date	Explanation	PR	Debit	Credit	Balance	
					Debit	Credit

Accounts Payable

Acct. No. __201__

Date	Explanation	PR	Debit	Credit	Balance	
					Debit	Credit

Notes Payable

Acct. No. __202__

Date	Explanation	PR	Debit	Credit	Balance	
					Debit	Credit

J. Southern, Drawing

Acct. No. __311__

Date	Explanation	PR	Debit	Credit	Balance	
					Debit	Credit

E6-26 (continued)

Purchases
Acct. No. __501__

Date	Explanation	PR	Debit	Credit	Balance Debit	Balance Credit

Purchases Discounts
Acct. No. __504__

Date	Explanation	PR	Debit	Credit	Balance Debit	Balance Credit

Rent Expense
Acct. No. __715__

Date	Explanation	PR	Debit	Credit	Balance Debit	Balance Credit

E6-26 (continued)

ACCOUNTS PAYABLE SUBSIDIARY LEDGER

A. Henry
Acct. No. ___5___

Date	Explanation	PR	Debit	Credit	Balance Debit	Balance Credit

S. Hughes
Acct. No. ___7___

Date	Explanation	PR	Debit	Credit	Balance Debit	Balance Credit

D. West
Acct. No. ___20___

Date	Explanation	PR	Debit	Credit	Balance Debit	Balance Credit

E6-27 Discovery of Journalizing Errors

_____
_____
_____
_____
_____
_____
_____
_____
_____
_____
_____
_____
_____
_____
_____
_____
_____
_____
_____
_____
_____
_____
_____
_____
_____
_____

E6-28 Identification of Journal Sources

1. _____	**6.**	**11.** _____
2. _____	**7.**	**12.** _____
3. _____	**8.**	**13.** _____
4. _____	**9.**	**14.** _____
5. _____	**10.**	

E6-29 Identifying the Source of Postings to the General Ledger

a. _____

b. _____

c. _____

d. _____

e. _____

f. _____

g. _____

h. _____

i. _____

j. _____

Name _____

Section _____

A AND B PROBLEMS

P6-30A or P6-30B Sales and Collection Transactions

Requirement 1

SALES JOURNAL

Page _____

Date	Sales Invoice No.	Account Debited	Terms	PR	Amount

P6-30A or P6-30B Requirement 1 (continued)

CASH RECEIPTS JOURNAL

Page _____

Date	Account Debited/Credited	PR	Debits			Credits		
			Cash	Sales Disc.	Other Accounts	Accounts Receivable	Sales	Other Accounts

P6-30A or P6-30B Requirement 1 (continued)

GENERAL JOURNAL

Date	Accounts and Explanations	PR	Debit	Credit

P6-30A or P6-30B (continued)

Requirements 2 and 3

GENERAL LEDGER

_____ Acct. No. _____

Date	Explanation	PR	Debit	Credit	Balance	
					Debit	Credit

_____ Acct. No. _____

Date	Explanation	PR	Debit	Credit	Balance	
					Debit	Credit

_____ Acct. No. _____

Date	Explanation	PR	Debit	Credit	Balance	
					Debit	Credit

P6-30A or P6-30B Requirements 2 and 3 (continued)

_____   Acct. No. _____

Date	Explanation	PR	Debit	Credit	Balance	
					Debit	**Credit**

_____   Acct. No. _____

Date	Explanation	PR	Debit	Credit	Balance	
					Debit	**Credit**

(P6-30A)

_____   Acct. No. _____

Date	Explanation	PR	Debit	Credit	Balance	
					Debit	**Credit**

P6-30A or P6-30B Requirements 2 and 3 (continued)

ACCOUNTS RECEIVABLE SUBSIDIARY LEDGER

_____   Acct. No. _____

Date	Explanation	PR	Debit	Credit	Balance	
					Debit	Credit

_____   Acct. No. _____

Date	Explanation	PR	Debit	Credit	Balance	
					Debit	Credit

_____   Acct. No. _____

Date	Explanation	PR	Debit	Credit	Balance	
					Debit	Credit

P6-30A or P6-30B Requirements 2 and 3 (continued)

_____ Acct. No. _____

Date	Explanation	PR	Debit	Credit	Balance Debit	Balance Credit

_____ Acct. No. _____

Date	Explanation	PR	Debit	Credit	Balance Debit	Balance Credit

(P6-30B)

_____ Acct. No. _____

Date	Explanation	PR	Debit	Credit	Balance Debit	Balance Credit

P6-31A or P6-31B Purchases and Payment Journal

Requirement 1

PURCHASES JOURNAL

Date	Account Credited	Terms	PR	Credit	Debits	
				Accounts Payable	Purchases	Office Supplies

P6-31A or P6-31B Requirement 1 (continued)

CASH PAYMENTS JOURNAL

Page _____

Date	Ck. No.	Account Debited/Credited	PR	Credits			Debits		
				Cash	Purch. Disc.	Other Accounts	Accounts Payable	Purchases	Other Accounts

GENERAL JOURNAL

Page _____

Date	Accounts and Explanations	PR	Debit	Credit

P6-31A or P6-31B (continued)

Requirements 2 and 3

GENERAL LEDGER

_____ Acct. No. _____

Date	Explanation	PR	Debit	Credit	Balance	
					Debit	Credit

_____ Acct. No. _____

Date	Explanation	PR	Debit	Credit	Balance	
					Debit	Credit

_____ Acct. No. _____

Date	Explanation	PR	Debit	Credit	Balance	
					Debit	Credit

P6-31A or P6-31B Requirements 2 and 3 (continued)

_____ Acct. No. _____

Date	Explanation	PR	Debit	Credit	Balance	
					Debit	Credit

_____ Acct. No. _____

Date	Explanation	PR	Debit	Credit	Balance	
					Debit	Credit

_____ Acct. No. _____

Date	Explanation	PR	Debit	Credit	Balance	
					Debit	Credit

ACCOUNTS PAYABLE SUBSIDIARY LEDGER

_____ Acct. No. _____

Date	Explanation	PR	Debit	Credit	Balance	
					Debit	Credit

P6-31A or P6-31B Requirements 2 and 3 (continued)

_____ Acct. No. _____

Date	Explanation	PR	Debit	Credit	Balance	
					Debit	Credit

_____ Acct. No. _____

Date	Explanation	PR	Debit	Credit	Balance	
					Debit	Credit

_____ Acct. No. _____

Date	Explanation	PR	Debit	Credit	Balance	
					Debit	Credit

P6-32A or P6-32B Journalizing and Posting Transactions in Special Journals

Requirement 1

PURCHASES JOURNAL
Page _____

Date		Account Credited	Terms	PR	Credit	Debits	
					Accounts Payable	Purchases	Office Supplies

SALES JOURNAL
Page _____

Date		Sales Invoice No.	Account Debited	Terms	PR	Amount

CASH PAYMENTS JOURNAL
Page _____

Date		Ck. No.	Account Debited/Credited	PR	Credits			Debits		
					Cash	Purch. Disc.	Other Accounts	Accounts Payable	Purchases	Other Accounts

(continued)

P6-32A or P6-32B Requirement 1 (continued)

Date	Ck. No.	Account Debited/Credited	PR	Credits			Debits		
				Cash	Purch. Disc.	Other Accounts	Accounts Payable	Purchases	Other Accounts

CASH RECEIPTS JOURNAL   Page _____

Date	Account Debited/Credited	PR	Debits			Credits		
			Cash	Sales Disc.	Other Accounts	Accounts Receivable	Sales	Other Accounts

GENERAL JOURNAL   Page _____

Date	Accounts and Explanations	PR	Debit	Credit

P6-32A or P6-32B (continued)

Requirements 2 and 3

GENERAL LEDGER

_____ Acct. No. _____

Date	Explanation	PR	Debit	Credit	Balance	
					Debit	**Credit**

_____ Acct. No. _____

Date	Explanation	PR	Debit	Credit	Balance	
					Debit	**Credit**

_____ Acct. No. _____

Date	Explanation	PR	Debit	Credit	Balance	
					Debit	**Credit**

_____ Acct. No. _____

Date	Explanation	PR	Debit	Credit	Balance	
					Debit	**Credit**

P6-32A or P6-32B Requirements 2 and 3 (continued)

_____ Acct. No. _____

Date	Explanation	PR	Debit	Credit	Balance	
					Debit	Credit

_____ Acct. No. _____

Date	Explanation	PR	Debit	Credit	Balance	
					Debit	Credit

_____ Acct. No. _____

Date	Explanation	PR	Debit	Credit	Balance	
					Debit	Credit

_____ Acct. No. _____

Date	Explanation	PR	Debit	Credit	Balance	
					Debit	Credit

P6-32A or P6-32B Requirements 2 and 3 (continued)

_____ Acct. No. _____

Date	Explanation	PR	Debit	Credit	Balance	
					Debit	Credit

_____ Aoot. No. _____

Date	Explanation	PR	Debit	Credit	Balance	
					Debit	Credit

(P6-32A)

_____ Acct. No. _____

Date	Explanation	PR	Debit	Credit	Balance	
					Debit	Credit

(P6-32A)

_____ Acct. No. _____

Date	Explanation	PR	Debit	Credit	Balance	
					Debit	Credit

P6-32A or P6-32B Requirements 2 and 3 (continued)

ACCOUNTS RECEIVABLE SUBSIDIARY LEDGER

Acct. No. _____

Date	Explanation	PR	Debit	Credit	Balance	
					Debit	Credit

Acct. No. _____

Date	Explanation	PR	Debit	Credit	Balance	
					Debit	Credit

P6-32A or P6-32B Requirements 2 and 3 (continued)

ACCOUNTS PAYABLE SUBSIDIARY LEDGER

_____ Acct. No. _____

Date	Explanation	PR	Debit	Credit	Balance Debit	Balance Credit

_____ Acct. No. _____

Date	Explanation	PR	Debit	Credit	Balance Debit	Balance Credit

_____ Acct. No. _____

Date	Explanation	PR	Debit	Credit	Balance Debit	Balance Credit

P6-32A or P6-32B (continued)

Requirement 4

Trial Balance

Acct. No.	Account Title	Debits	Credits

Schedule of Accounts Receivable

Acct. No.	Account Title	Amount

Schedule of Accounts Payable

Acct. No.	Account Title	Amount

P6-33A or P6-33B Journalizing to All Journals

Requirements 1 and 2

GENERAL JOURNAL

Page _____

Date	Accounts and Explanations	PR	Debit	Credit

P6-33A or P6-33B Requirements 1 and 2 (continued)

CASH RECEIPTS JOURNAL

Page_____

Date	Account Debited/Credited	PR	Debits			Credits		
			Cash	Sales Disc.	Other Accounts	Accounts Receivable	Sales	Other Accounts

P6-33A or P6-33B Requirements 1 and 2 (continued)

CASH PAYMENTS JOURNAL

Page _____

Date	Ck. No.	Account Debited/Credited	PR	Credits			Debits		
				Cash	Purch. Disc.	Other Accounts	Accounts Payable	Purchases	Other Accounts

P6-33A or P6-33B Requirements 1 and 2 (continued)

SALES JOURNAL

Page _____

Date		Sales Invoice No.	Account Debited	Terms	PR	Amount

PURCHASES JOURNAL

Page _____

Date		Account Credited	Terms	PR	Credit	Debits	
					Accounts Payable	Purchases	Office Supplies

P6-34A or P6-34B   Complex Cash Receipts and Payment Transactions

CASH PAYMENTS JOURNAL   Page _____

Date	Ck. No.	Account Debited/Credited	PR	Credits			Debits		
				Cash	Purch. Disc.	Other Accounts	Accounts Payable	Purchases	Other Accounts

CASH RECEIPTS JOURNAL   Page _____

Date	Account Debited/Credited	PR	Debits			Credits		
			Cash	Sales Disc.	Other Accounts	Accounts Receivable	Sales	Other Accounts

P6-35A Reconstruction of Controlling Account from Subsidiary Postings or

P6-35B Reconstruction of Controlling Account from Subsidiary Ledger

Requirement 1

GENERAL LEDGER

_____ Acct No. _____

Date	Explanation	PR	Debit	Credit	Balance	
					Debit	Credit

Requirement 2 (P6-35A)

_____

_____

_____

Acct. No.	Account Title	Amount

P6-35A or P6-35B (continued)

Requirement 2 (P6-35B)

_____
_____
_____

6-36A or P6-36B Reconstruction of Special Journal Totals from General Ledger Accounts

PURCHASES JOURNAL   Page _____

| Date | | Account Credited | Terms | PR | Credit | Debits | |
					Accounts Payable	Purchases	Office Supplies

SALES JOURNAL   Page _____

Date		Sales Invoice No.	Account Debited	Terms	PR	Amount

CASH PAYMENTS JOURNAL   Page _____

| Date | Ck. No. | Account Debited/Credited | PR | Credits | | | Debits | | |
				Cash	Purch. Disc.	Other Accounts	Accounts Payable	Purchases	Other Accounts

CASH RECEIPTS JOURNAL   Page _____

| Date | | Account Debited/Credited | PR | Debits | | | Credits | | |
				Cash	Sales Disc.	Other Accounts	Accounts Receivable	Sales	Other Accounts

PRACTICE CASE
Special Journals

Requirement 1

PURCHASES JOURNAL   Page _____

Date	Account Credited	Terms	PR	Credit Accounts Payable	Debits Purchases	Debits Office Supplies

SALES JOURNAL   Page _____

Date	Sales Invoice No.	Account Debited	Terms	PR	Amount

Practice Case Requirement 1 (continued)

CASH PAYMENTS JOURNAL   Page _____

| Date | Ck. No. | Account Debited/Credited | PR | Credits | | | Debits | | |
				Cash	Purch. Disc.	Other Accounts	Accounts Payable	Purchases	Other Accounts

CASH RECEIPTS JOURNAL   Page _____

| Date | Account Debited/Credited | PR | Debits | | | Credits | | |
			Cash	Sales Disc.	Other Accounts	Accounts Receivable	Sales	Other Accounts

Practice Case Requirement 1 (continued)

GENERAL JOURNAL

Date	Accounts and Explanations	PR	Debit	Credit

Name _____

Section _____

Practice Case (continued)

Requirements 2 and 3

GENERAL LEDGER
Cash
Acct. No. __101__

Date	Explanation	PR	Debit	Credit	Balance Debit	Balance Credit

Accounts Receivable
Acct. No. __111__

Date	Explanation	PR	Debit	Credit	Balance Debit	Balance Credit

Office Supplies
Acct. No. __135__

Date	Explanation	PR	Debit	Credit	Balance Debit	Balance Credit

Accounts Payable
Acct. No. __201__

Date	Explanation	PR	Debit	Credit	Balance Debit	Balance Credit

Practice Case Requirements 2 and 3 (continued)

Notes Payable
Acct. No. __202__

Date	Explanation	PR	Debit	Credit	Balance Debit	Balance Credit

Interest Payable
Acct. No. _____

Date	Explanation	PR	Debit	Credit	Balance Debit	Balance Credit

D. Skee, Capital
Acct. No. __301__

Date	Explanation	PR	Debit	Credit	Balance Debit	Balance Credit

Sales
Acct. No. __401__

Date	Explanation	PR	Debit	Credit	Balance Debit	Balance Credit

Practice Case Requirements 2 and 3 (continued)

Sales Discounts

Acct. No. __403__

Date	Explanation	PR	Debit	Credit	Balance Debit	Balance Credit

Purchases

Acct. No. __501__

Date	Explanation	PR	Debit	Credit	Balance Debit	Balance Credit

Transportation In

Acct. No. __502__

Date	Explanation	PR	Debit	Credit	Balance Debit	Balance Credit

Purchases Returns and Allowances

Acct. No. __503__

Date	Explanation	PR	Debit	Credit	Balance Debit	Balance Credit

Practice Case Requirements 2 and 3 (continued)

Purchases Discounts

Acct. No. __504__

Date	Explanation	PR	Debit	Credit	Balance Debit	Balance Credit

Rent Expense

Acct. No. __615__

Date	Explanation	PR	Debit	Credit	Balance Debit	Balance Credit

Advertising Expense

Acct. No. __616__

Date	Explanation	PR	Debit	Credit	Balance Debit	Balance Credit

Transportation Out Expense

Acct. No. __617__

Date	Explanation	PR	Debit	Credit	Balance Debit	Balance Credit

Practice Case Requirements 2 and 3 (continued)

Interest Expense

Acct. No. __852__

Date	Explanation	PR	Debit	Credit	Balance Debit	Balance Credit

ACCOUNTS RECEIVABLE SUBSIDIARY LEDGER

D. Adel

Acct. No. __1__

Date	Explanation	PR	Debit	Credit	Balance Debit	Balance Credit

S. Ipsen

Acct. No. __7__

Date	Explanation	PR	Debit	Credit	Balance Debit	Balance Credit

Practice Case Requirements 2 and 3 (continued)

ACCOUNTS PAYABLE SUBSIDIARY LEDGER

C. Bluff Company
Acct. No. ___3___

Date	Explanation	PR	Debit	Credit	Balance	
					Debit	Credit

Office Outfitters
Acct. No. ___5___

Date	Explanation	PR	Debit	Credit	Balance	
					Debit	Credit

Import, Inc.
Acct. No. ___8___

Date	Explanation	PR	Debit	Credit	Balance	
					Debit	Credit

Practice Case (continued)

Requirement 4

Trial Balance

Acct. No.	Account Title	Debits	Credits

Practice Case Requirement 4 (continued)

Schedule of Accounts Receivable

Schedule of Accounts Payable

Practice Case (continued)

Requirement 5

Income Statement

Name _____

Section _____

Practice Case Requirement 5 (continued)

Statement of Owner's Equity

Balance Sheet

6-61

Practice Case (continued)

Requirement 6

_____
_____
_____
_____
_____
_____
_____
_____
_____
_____
_____
_____
_____
_____
_____
_____
_____
_____

BUSINESS DECISION AND COMMUNICATION PROBLEM

Design an Accounting System

_____

Name _____

Section _____

Business Decision and Communication Problem (continued)

Name _____

Section _____

Business Decision and Communication Problem (continued)

_____
_____
_____
_____
_____
_____
_____
_____
_____
_____
_____
_____
_____
_____
_____
_____
_____
_____
_____
_____
_____
_____
_____
_____
_____
_____
_____
_____
_____
_____
_____
_____
_____
_____
_____
_____
_____
_____
_____
_____

Name _____

Section _____

ETHICAL DILEMMA

Altering Source Documents

Section _____

CHAPTER 7
Payroll System

EXERCISES
E7-12 Computing Gross Pay

E7-13 Using Income Tax Withholding Table

E7-14 Computing FICA Tax Withheld

7-1

Copyright © 1992 by Harcourt Brace Jovanovich, Inc. All rights reserved.

E7-15 Computing FICA Tax Expense

a.

b.

E7-16 Computing FUTA Tax Expense

E7-17 Recording a Payroll, Payment, and Employer's Tax Expense

a.

GENERAL JOURNAL

Page _____

Date	Accounts and Explanations	PR	Debit	Credit

b.

GENERAL JOURNAL

Page _____

Date	Accounts and Explanations	PR	Debit	Credit

E7-17 (continued)

c.

GENERAL JOURNAL

Page _____

Date	Accounts and Explanations	PR	Debit	Credit

E7-18 Computing Payroll Tax Expense

E7-19 FICA Tax Computations at the Wage Base

E7-20 FUTA Tax Computations at the Wage Base

E7-21 Total Cost of an Employee

E7-22 Recognizing Expense and Payment of Vacation Pay

a.

GENERAL JOURNAL

Date	Accounts and Explanations	PR	Debit	Credit

b.

GENERAL JOURNAL

Date	Accounts and Explanations	PR	Debit	Credit

E7-23 Internal Control over Payroll and Other Uses of Data

a.

_____
_____
_____
_____
_____
_____
_____
_____
_____
_____
_____
_____
_____
_____
_____
_____
_____
_____
_____
_____
_____
_____
_____
_____
_____

E7-23 (continued)

b.

_____
_____
_____
_____
_____
_____
_____
_____
_____
_____
_____
_____
_____
_____
_____
_____
_____
_____
_____
_____
_____

c.

_____
_____
_____
_____
_____
_____
_____
_____
_____
_____
_____
_____

A AND B PROBLEMS

P7-24A or P7-24B Computing Gross and Net Pay with Deductions Given

PAYROLL REGISTER   **WEEK ENDED** _____

Employee Name	Hours Worked	Rate	Regular Pay	Overtime Pay	Overtime Premium	Total Gross Pay	Deductions				Net Pay
							Income Tax	FICA	Other	Total	

Name _____

Section _____

P7-25A or P7-25B Journalizing Payroll Transactions: Amounts Given

Requirement 1

GENERAL JOURNAL

Date	Accounts and Explanations	PR	Debit	Credit

Requirement 2

GENERAL JOURNAL

Date	Accounts and Explanations	PR	Debit	Credit

Name _____

Section _____

P7-26A or P7-26B   Completing a Payroll Register and Recording the Payroll
Requirement 1.

PAYROLL REGISTER   WEEK ENDED _____

| Employee Name | Rate | Hours Worked | Regular and Over-time Pay | Overtime Premium | Total Gross Pay | FICA | Income Tax | | Union Dues | Med. Ins. | Pen. Fund | Total | Net Pay |
							Federal	State					

7-13

P7-26A or P7-26B Completing a Payroll Register and Recording the Payroll

Requirement 2

GENERAL JOURNAL   Page _____

Date	Accounts and Explanations	PR	Debit	Credit

P7-27A or P7-27B Preparing a Payroll Register and Entries to Record the Payroll, Its Payment, and Employer Taxes

Requirement 1

| Employee Name | Gross Pay | Deductions | | | Total | Net Pay |
		FICA	Federal Income Tax	Health Plan		

Requirement 2

GENERAL JOURNAL

Page _____

Date	Accounts and Explanations	PR	Debit	Credit

P7-27A or P7-27B (continued)

Requirement 3

GENERAL JOURNAL   Page _____

Date	Accounts and Explanations	PR	Debit	Credit

Requirement 4

GENERAL JOURNAL   Page _____

Date	Accounts and Explanations	PR	Debit	Credit

P7-28A or P7-28B Computing Payroll and Taxes at Various Wage Bases and Recording the Payroll

Requirement 1

GENERAL JOURNAL

Page _____

Date	Accounts and Explanations	PR	Debit	Credit

Requirement 2

GENERAL JOURNAL

Page _____

Date	Accounts and Explanations	PR	Debit	Credit

P7-28A or P7-28B (continued)

Requirement 3

Page _____

GENERAL JOURNAL

Date	Accounts and Explanations	PR	Debit	Credit

P7-29A or P7-29B Liability for Vacation Pay

Requirement 1

GENERAL JOURNAL

Page _____

Date	Accounts and Explanations	PR	Debit	Credit

Requirement 2

GENERAL JOURNAL

Page _____

Date	Accounts and Explanations	PR	Debit	Credit

Requirement 3

_____
_____
_____
_____
_____
_____
_____
_____
_____
_____
_____
_____
_____

P7-30A or P7-30B Internal Control of Payroll

PRACTICE CASE

Payroll System

Requirement 1

PAYROLL REGISTER   **WEEK ENDED** _____

Employee Name	Gross Pay	Deductions					Net Pay
		FICA	Federal Income Tax	State Income Tax	Health Plan	Total	

Practice Case (continued)

Requirement 2

GENERAL JOURNAL   Page _____

Date	Accounts and Explanations	PR	Debit	Credit

Requirement 3

GENERAL JOURNAL   Page _____

Date	Accounts and Explanations	PR	Debit	Credit

Practice Case (continued)

Requirement 4

GENERAL JOURNAL　　　　　　　　　Page _____

Date	Accounts and Explanations	PR	Debit	Credit

Requirement 5

GENERAL JOURNAL　　　　　　　　　Page _____

Date	Accounts and Explanations	PR	Debit	Credit

BUSINESS DECISION AND COMMUNICATION PROBLEM

Remittance of Taxes

Name _____

Section _____

Business Decision and Communication Problem (continued)

Name _____

Section _____

ETHICAL DILEMMA

Payroll Control

CHAPTER 8
Internal Control and Cash

EXERCISES
E8-15 Internal Control

_____
_____
_____
_____
_____
_____
_____
_____
_____
_____
_____
_____
_____
_____
_____
_____
_____
_____
_____
_____
_____
_____
_____
_____
_____
_____
_____
_____
_____

E8-16 Petty Cash Transactions

1.

GENERAL JOURNAL
Page _____

Date		Accounts and Explanations	PR	Debit	Credit

2.

GENERAL JOURNAL
Page _____

Date		Accounts and Explanations	PR	Debit	Credit

3.

_____
_____
_____
_____
_____
_____
_____
_____
_____
_____

E8-17 Cash Over and Short

_____
_____
_____
_____
_____
_____

GENERAL JOURNAL   Page _____

Date	Accounts and Explanations	PR	Debit	Credit

E8-18 Items on the Bank Reconciliation

1. _____	5. _____	9. _____
2. _____	6. _____	10. _____
3. _____	7. _____	
4. _____	8. _____	

E8-19 Simple Bank Reconciliation

E8-20 Recording Reconciliation Items

GENERAL JOURNAL

Date	Accounts and Explanations	PR	Debit	Credit

E8-21 Finding Reconciliation Errors

E8-22 Bank Reconciliation and Journal Entries

E8-22 (continued)

GENERAL JOURNAL

Date	Accounts and Explanations	PR	Debit	Credit

Name _____

Section _____

E8-23 Voucher Register Transactions

VOUCHER REGISTER

Date	Vou. No.	Name	Paid Date	Paid Ck. No.	Credit Vouchers Payable	Debit Purchs.	Debit Misc. Selling Expense	Debit Misc. General Expense	Debit Other Accts.	Debit PR	Debit Amt.

8-8

F8-24 Check Register Transactions

CHECK REGISTER							
Date	Voucher No.	Name	Check No.	Vouchers Payable Dr.	Purch. Disc. Cr.	Cash Cr.	

8-9

E8-25 Voucher Cancellation

VOUCHER REGISTER

Date	Voucher No.	Name	Paid		Credit	Debit					
			Date	Ck. No.	Vouchers Payable	Purchs.	Misc. Selling Expense	Misc. General Expense	Other Accts.	PR	Amt.

CHECK REGISTER

Date	Voucher No.	Name	Check No.	Vouchers Payable Dr.	Purch. Disc. Cr.	Cash Cr.

E8-26 Partial Payment: Discount Allowed

VOUCHER REGISTER

| Date | Voucher No. | Name | Paid | | Credit | Debit | | | | | |
			Date	Ck. No.	Vouchers Payable	Purchs.	Misc. Selling Expense	Misc. General Expense	Other Accts.	PR	Amt.

CHECK REGISTER

Date	Voucher No.	Name	Check No.	Vouchers Payable Dr.	Purch. Disc. Cr.	Cash Cr.

A AND B PROBLEMS

P8-27A or P8-27B Internal Control System (Based on an Actual Occurrence)

Requirement 1

_____

P8-27A or P8-27B (continued)

Requirement 2

_____
_____
_____
_____
_____
_____
_____
_____
_____
_____
_____
_____
_____
_____
_____
_____
_____
_____
_____
_____
_____
_____
_____
_____
_____
_____
_____
_____
_____
_____
_____
_____
_____
_____
_____
_____
_____
_____

P8-28A or P8-28B Petty Cash Fund

Requirement 1

GENERAL JOURNAL

Page _____

Date	Accounts and Explanations	PR	Debit	Credit

Requirement 2

GENERAL JOURNAL

Page _____

Date	Accounts and Explanations	PR	Debit	Credit

P8-28A or P8-28B (continued)

Requirement 3

GENERAL JOURNAL   Page _____

Date	Accounts and Explanations	PR	Debit	Credit

P8-29A or P8-29B Bank Reconciliation: Routine Items

Requirement 1

_____

_____

_____

P8-29A or P8-29B (continued)

Requirement 2

GENERAL JOURNAL

Date	Accounts and Explanations	PR	Debit	Credit

P8-30A or P8-30B Bank Reconciliation: Tracing Items to Statements

Requirement 1

_____
_____
_____

P8-30A or P8-30B (continued)

Requirement 2

GENERAL JOURNAL   Page _____

Date	Accounts and Explanations	PR	Debit	Credit

P8-31A or P8-31B Bank Reconciliation: Based on Bank Statement and Company Records

Requirement 1

_____
_____
_____

P8-31A or P8-31B (continued)

Requirement 2

GENERAL JOURNAL

Date	Accounts and Explanations	PR	Debit	Credit

P8-32A or P8-32B Voucher Register and Check Register

Requirement 1

(continued)

VOUCHER REGISTER

Date	Voucher No.	Name	Paid		Credit	Debit						
			Date	Ck. No.	Vouchers Payable	Purchs.	Misc. Selling Expense	Misc. General Expense	Other Accts.	PR	Amt.	

P8-32A or P8-32B Requirement 1 (continued)

Date	Voucher No.	Name	Paid Date	Paid Ck. No.	Credit Vouchers Payable	Purchs.	Debit Misc. Selling Expense	Debit Misc. General Expense	Debit Other Accts.	PR	Amt.

VOUCHER REGISTER

Name _____

Section _____

P8-32A or P8-32B Requirement 1 (continued)

		CHECK REGISTER				Page 1
Date	Voucher No.	Name	Check No.	Vouchers Payable Dr.	Purch. Disc. Cr.	Cash Cr.

Name _____

Section _____

P8-32A or P8-32B Requirement 1 (continued)

GENERAL JOURNAL   Page _____

Date	Accounts and Explanations	PR	Debit	Credit

Requirement 2

GENERAL LEDGER
Voucher's Payable   Acct. No. __206__

Date	Explanation	PR	Debit	Credit	Balance Debit	Balance Credit

8-26

P8-32A or P8-32B (continued)

Requirement 3

_____
_____
_____

Voucher No.	Name	Amount

P8-33A Imprest Change Fund

Requirement 1a and 1b

GENERAL JOURNAL

Date	Accounts and Explanations	PR	Debit	Credit

Requirement 2

_____

P8-33B Determining a Cash Theft

Requirement 1

P8-33B (continued)

Requirement 2

Requirement 3

PRACTICE CASE

Internal Control and Cash Transactions

Requirement 1

_____

_____

_____

Name _____

Section _____

Practice Case (continued)

Requirement 2

Practice Case (continued)

Requirement 3

GENERAL JOURNAL

Date	Accounts and Explanations	PR	Debit	Credit

Practice Case (continued)

Requirement 4

_____
_____
_____
_____
_____
_____
_____
_____
_____
_____
_____
_____
_____
_____
_____
_____
_____
_____
_____
_____
_____

Name _____

Section _____

BUSINESS DECISION AND COMMUNICATION PROBLEM

Internal Control over Cash

Name _____

Section _____

Business Decision and Communication Problem (continued)

ETHICAL DILEMMA

Theft by the Petty Cash Clerk

_____
_____
_____
_____
_____
_____
_____
_____
_____
_____
_____
_____
_____
_____
_____
_____
_____
_____
_____
_____
_____
_____
_____
_____
_____
_____
_____
_____
_____
_____
_____
_____
_____
_____
_____
_____
_____
_____
_____
_____

CHAPTER 9
Accounts Receivable and Bad Debt Expense

EXERCISES
E9-16 Balance Sheet Classification of Receivables

1.

_____
Partial Balance Sheet

E9-16 (continued)

2.

_____
_____
_____
_____
_____
_____
_____
_____
_____
_____
_____
_____
_____
_____
_____
_____
_____
_____
_____
_____
_____
_____
_____
_____
_____
_____
_____
_____
_____
_____
_____
_____
_____
_____
_____
_____
_____
_____
_____
_____

E9-17 Journalizing Entries under the Allowance Method

GENERAL JOURNAL

Date	Accounts and Explanations	PR	Debit	Credit

E9-18 Recording Bad Debts Expense by Use of the Allowance Method

GENERAL JOURNAL

Date	Accounts and Explanations	PR	Debit	Credit

E9-19 Recording Bad Debts by Use of the Allowance Method

GENERAL JOURNAL

Date	Accounts and Explanations	PR	Debit	Credit

E9-20 Recording Bad Debts Expense, Write-off, and Balance Sheet Presentation under the Allowance Method

1.

GENERAL JOURNAL

Date	Accounts and Explanations	PR	Debit	Credit

2.

Partial Balance Sheet

3.

GENERAL JOURNAL

Date	Accounts and Explanations	PR	Debit	Credit

E9-20 (continued)

4.

Partial Balance Sheet

E9-21 Aging Accounts Receivable and Recording Bad Debts Expense under the Allowance Method

1.

Analysis of Accounts Receivable by Age

Customer's Name	Total Balance	Not Yet Due	Items Past Due				
			1-30 Days	31-60 Days	61-90 Days	91-120 Days	121-365 Days

E9-21 (continued)

2.

_____
_____
_____
_____
_____
_____
_____
_____
_____
_____
_____
_____
_____
_____
_____
_____
_____
_____
_____

3.

GENERAL JOURNAL

Date	Accounts and Explanations	PR	Debit	Credit

Name _____

Section _____

E9-22 Journalizing Entries under the Direct Write-off Method

GENERAL JOURNAL

Date	Accounts and Explanations	PR	Debit	Credit

E9-23 Comparing the Allowance and Direct Write-off Methods

1.

E9-23 (continued)

2.

E9-24 Accounting for Credit Card Sales

GENERAL JOURNAL

Date	Accounts and Explanations	PR	Debit	Credit

E9-25 Balance Sheet Disclosure of Receivables with Credit Balances

Partial Balance Sheet

E9-26 Internal Control of Accounts Receivable

_____
_____
_____
_____
_____
_____
_____
_____
_____
_____
_____
_____
_____
_____
_____
_____
_____
_____
_____
_____
_____
_____
_____
_____
_____
_____
_____

Name _____

Section _____

E9-27 Analyzing Real-life Entries to Allowance Account

GENERAL JOURNAL

Date	Accounts and Explanations	PR	Debit	Credit

E9-28 Chapter Integrating and Review Exercise: Computing Cash Received from Customers

A AND B PROBLEMS

P9-29A or P9-29B Journalizing Entries under the Allowance Method

GENERAL JOURNAL

Date	Accounts and Explanations	PR	Debit	Credit

Name _____

Section _____

P9-30A or P9-30B Journalizing Entries under the Allowance Method: Using Estimates Based on Both Sales and Receivables

Requirement 1

GENERAL JOURNAL

Date	Accounts and Explanations	PR	Debit	Credit

(continued)

9-19

P9-30A or P9-30B Requirement 1 (continued)

Date	Accounts and Explanations	PR	Debit	Credit

P9-30A or P9-30B (continued)

Requirement 2

GENERAL LEDGER

_____ Acct. No. _____

Date	Explanation	PR	Debit	Credit	Balance	
					Debit	Credit

P9-31A or P9-31B Recording Various Accounts Receivable Transactions Using the Allowance Method

Requirement 1

GENERAL JOURNAL

Page _____

Date	Accounts and Explanations	PR	Debit	Credit

(continued)

9-23

P9-31A or P9-31B   Requirement 1 (continued)

Date	Accounts and Explanations	PR	Debit	Credit

(continued)

P9-31A or P9-31B Requirement 1 (continued)

Date	Accounts and Explanations	PR	Debit	Credit

P9-31A or P9-31B (continued)

Requirement 2

GENERAL LEDGER

_____   Acct. No. _____

Date	Explanation	PR	Debit	Credit	Balance	
					Debit	Credit

_____   Acct. No. _____

Date	Explanation	PR	Debit	Credit	Balance	
					Debit	Credit

9-26

P9-31A or P9-31B Requirement 2 (continued)

Accounts Receivable Subsidiary Ledger

_____ Acct. _____

Date	Explanation	PR	Debit	Credit	Balance	
					Debit	**Credit**

_____ Acct. _____

Date	Explanation	PR	Debit	Credit	Balance	
					Debit	**Credit**

_____ Acct. _____

Date	Explanation	PR	Debit	Credit	Balance	
					Debit	**Credit**

_____ Acct. _____

Date	Explanation	PR	Debit	Credit	Balance	
					Debit	**Credit**

P9-31A or P9-31B Requirement 2 (continued)

Accounts Receivable Subsidiary Ledger

_____ Acct. _____

Date	Explanation	PR	Debit	Credit	Balance	
					Debit	Credit

_____ Acct. _____

Date	Explanation	PR	Debit	Credit	Balance	
					Debit	Credit

Requirement 3

Schedule of Accounts Receivable

P9-32A or P9-32B Aging Accounts Receivable and Recording Bad Debit Expense

Requirement 1

Analysis of Accounts Receivable by Age

Customer's Name	Total Balance	Not Yet Due	Items Past Due			
			1-30 Days	31-60 Days	61-90 Days	Over 90 Days

P9-32A or P9-32B (continued)

Requirement 2

_____
_____
_____
_____
_____
_____
_____
_____
_____
_____
_____
_____
_____
_____
_____
_____
_____
_____
_____

Requirement 3

GENERAL JOURNAL

Date	Accounts and Explanations	PR	Debit	Credit

P9-33A **Journalizing Entries and Preparing an Income Statement under the Direct Write-off Method or**

P9-33B **Journalizing Entries and Preparing an Income Statement under the Allowance Method**

Requirement 1

GENERAL JOURNAL

Date	Accounts and Explanations	PR	Debit	Credit

Name _____

Section _____

P9-33A or P9-33B (continued)

Requirement 2

<u>Income Statement</u>

Requirement 3

P9-34A or P9-34B Comparing the Allowance Method with the Direct Write-off Method

Requirement 1

GENERAL LEDGER

_____ Acct. No. _____

Date	Explanation	PR	Debit	Credit	Balance Debit	Balance Credit

_____ Acct. No. _____

Date	Explanation	PR	Debit	Credit	Balance Debit	Balance Credit

9-33

P9-34A or P9-34B (continued)

Requirement 2

_____
_____
_____
_____
_____
_____
_____
_____
_____
_____
_____
_____

P9-35A Real-life Comparison of Allowance and Direct Write-off Method for Delta Air Lines, Inc.

Requirement 1

_____
_____
_____
_____
_____
_____

GENERAL JOURNAL

Date	Accounts and Explanations	PR	Debit	Credit

Requirement 2

_____
_____
_____
_____
_____
_____
_____
_____
_____
_____
_____

P9-35A Requirement 2 (continued)

GENERAL JOURNAL

Date	Accounts and Explanations	PR	Debit	Credit

Requirement 3

P9-35B Real-life Comparison of the Allowance and Direct Write-off Methods for Mattel, Inc.

_____

_____

_____

_____

_____

_____

_____

_____

_____

_____

_____

_____

_____

_____

_____

_____

_____

_____

_____

_____

_____

_____

_____

_____

_____

_____

_____

_____

_____

_____

_____

PRACTICE CASE

Accounts Receivable and Bad Debts Expense

Requirement 1

GENERAL JOURNAL

Date	Accounts and Explanations	PR	Debit	Credit

(continued)

Practice Case Requirement 1 (continued)

Date	Accounts and Explanations	PR	Debit	Credit

(continued)

Name _____

Section _____

Practice Case Requirement 1 (continued)

Date	Accounts and Explanations	PR	Debit	Credit

Requirement 2

9-41

Practice Case Requirement 2 (continued)

Requirement 3

Name _____

Section _____

BUSINESS DECISION AND COMMUNICATION PROBLEM

Effect of Alternative Methods for Bad Debts on Financial Statements

1.

Business Decision and Communication Problem (continued)

2.

_____
_____
_____
_____
_____
_____
_____
_____
_____
_____
_____
_____
_____
_____
_____
_____
_____
_____
_____
_____
_____

_____
_____
_____

Business Decision and Communication Problem (continued)

3.

_____
_____
_____
_____
_____
_____
_____
_____
_____
_____
_____
_____
_____
_____
_____
_____
_____
_____
_____
_____
_____
_____
_____
_____
_____
_____
_____
_____
_____
_____
_____
_____

ETHICAL DILEMMA

Disclose to Casino Customers That Some Gambling Debts Will Not Be Collected?

_____

_____

_____

_____

_____

_____

_____

_____

_____

_____

_____

_____

_____

_____

_____

_____

_____

_____

_____

_____

_____

_____

_____

_____

_____

_____

_____

_____

_____

_____

_____

_____

_____

_____

_____

_____

_____

_____

_____

_____

_____

_____

CHAPTER 10
Short-term Financing

EXERCISES
E10-12 Determining Maturity Date of Notes

_____
_____
_____
_____
_____
_____
_____
_____
_____
_____
_____
_____
_____
_____
_____
_____
_____
_____
_____
_____
_____
_____

E10-13 Determining Maturity Value of Notes

_____
_____
_____
_____
_____
_____
_____
_____
_____
_____
_____
_____
_____
_____
_____
_____
_____

E10-14 Calculating Effective Interest Rates

_____

_____

_____

_____

_____

_____

_____

_____

_____

_____

_____

_____

_____

_____

_____

_____

_____

_____

_____

_____

_____

_____

_____

_____

E10-15 Recording Notes Payable Transactions with Interest on Face Value

GENERAL JOURNAL

Date	Accounts and Explanations	PR	Debit	Credit

(continued)

E10-15 (continued)

Date		Accounts and Explanations	PR	Debit	Credit

(continued)

E10-15 (continued)

Date		Accounts and Explanations	PR	Debit	Credit

E10-16 Calculating and Recording Interest on Notes Payable

_____
_____
_____
_____
_____
_____
_____
_____
_____
_____
_____

GENERAL JOURNAL

Date		Accounts and Explanations	PR	Debit	Credit

E10-17 Recording Notes Payable Discounted at Face Value

GENERAL JOURNAL

Date	Accounts and Explanations	PR	Debit	Credit

(continued)

E10-17 (continued)

Date	Accounts and Explanations	PR	Debit	Credit

E10-18 Recording Issuance of Notes to Borrow from Banks and Calculating Effective Interest Rates

1.

GENERAL JOURNAL

Date	Accounts and Explanations	PR	Debit	Credit

(continued)

E10-18 (continued)

Date	Accounts and Explanations	PR	Debit	Credit

E10-18 (continued)

2.

_____

_____

_____

_____

_____

_____

_____

_____

_____

_____

_____

_____

_____

_____

_____

_____

Name _____

Section _____

E10-19 Recording Notes Receivable Transactions

GENERAL JOURNAL

Date	Accounts and Explanations	PR	Debit	Credit

(continued)

E10-19 (continued)

Date		Accounts and Explanations	PR	Debit	Credit

E10-20 Calculating and Recording Accrued Interest on Notes Receivable

_____
_____
_____
_____
_____
_____
_____
_____
_____
_____
_____

GENERAL JOURNAL

Date	Accounts and Explanations	PR	Debit	Credit

Name _____

Section _____

E10-21 Discounting a Customer's Note Receivable Paid by the Customer

GENERAL JOURNAL

Date	Accounts and Explanations	PR	Debit	Credit

E10-22 Discounting a Customer's Note Receivable Dishonored by the Customer

GENERAL JOURNAL

Date	Accounts and Explanations	PR	Debit	Credit

(continued)

E10-22 (continued)

Date	Accounts and Explanations	PR	Debit	Credit

Name _____

Section _____

E10-23 Recording Note Transaction: Maker and Payee

Books of Joe Link

GENERAL JOURNAL

Date	Accounts and Explanations	PR	Debit	Credit

E10-23 (continued)

Books of Peg Fay

GENERAL JOURNAL

Date	Accounts and Explanations	PR	Debit	Credit

E10-24 Describing Transactions from Account Data

_____
_____
_____
_____
_____
_____
_____
_____
_____
_____
_____
_____
_____
_____
_____
_____
_____
_____
_____
_____
_____
_____
_____
_____
_____

A AND B PROBLEMS

P10-25A Calculating and Recording Accrued Interest on Notes Payable

_____
_____
_____
_____
_____
_____
_____
_____
_____
_____
_____

GENERAL JOURNAL

Date	Accounts and Explanations	PR	Debit	Credit

P10-25B Calculating and Recording Accrued Interest on Notes Receivable

_____
_____
_____
_____
_____
_____
_____
_____
_____
_____
_____

GENERAL JOURNAL

Date	Accounts and Explanations	PR	Debit	Credit

P10-26A or P10-26B Determining Approximate APR

_____
_____
_____
_____
_____
_____
_____
_____
_____
_____
_____
_____
_____
_____
_____
_____
_____
_____
_____
_____
_____
_____
_____
_____

P10-27A or P10-27B Recording Notes Payable Transactions
GENERAL JOURNAL

Date	Accounts and Explanations	PR	Debit	Credit

(continued)

P10-27A or P10-27B (continued)

Date		Accounts and Explanations	PR	Debit	Credit

(continued)

Name _____

Section _____

P10-27A or P10-27B (continued)

Date	Accounts and Explanations	PR	Debit	Credit

10-29

P10-28A or P10-28B Determining Cost of Credit

Requirement 1

_____
_____
_____
_____
_____
_____
_____
_____
_____
_____
_____
_____
_____

Requirement 2

_____
_____
_____
_____
_____
_____
_____
_____
_____
_____
_____
_____
_____
_____
_____
_____
_____
_____

P10-29A or P10-29B Recording Notes Receivable Transactions

GENERAL JOURNAL

Date	Accounts and Explanations	PR	Debit	Credit

(continued)

P10-29A or P10-29B (continued)

Date	Accounts and Explanations	PR	Debit	Credit

(continued)

P10-29A or P10-29B (continued)

Date	Accounts and Explanations	PR	Debit	Credit

10-35

P10-30A Comprehensive Notes Receivable Transactions or

P10-30B Comprehensive Notes Receivable and Notes Payable Transactions

GENERAL JOURNAL

Date	Accounts and Explanations	PR	Debit	Credit

(continued)

P10-30A or P10-30B (continued)

Date	Accounts and Explanations	PR	Debit	Credit

(continued)

P10-30A or P10-30B (continued)

Date	Accounts and Explanations	PR	Debit	Credit

(continued)

10-39

P10-30A or P10-30B (continued)

Date	Accounts and Explanations	PR	Debit	Credit

P10-31A Interpretation of Short-term Borrowing and Credit Arrangement Note for The Coca-Cola Company

Requirement 1

_____
_____
_____
_____
_____
_____
_____
_____
_____
_____
_____
_____
_____
_____
_____
_____

Requirement 2

_____
_____
_____
_____
_____
_____
_____
_____
_____
_____
_____
_____
_____
_____
_____
_____
_____

P10-31B Selecting Best Source of Short-term Credit

_____
_____
_____
_____
_____
_____
_____
_____
_____
_____
_____
_____
_____
_____
_____
_____
_____
_____
_____
_____
_____
_____
_____
_____
_____
_____
_____
_____

Name _____

Section _____

PRACTICE CASE

Short-term Financing

GENERAL JOURNAL

Date	Accounts and Explanations	PR	Debit	Credit

(continued)

Practice Case (continued)

Date	Accounts and Explanations	PR	Debit	Credit

(continued)

10-46

Name _____

Section _____

Practice Case (continued)

Date	Accounts and Explanations	PR	Debit	Credit

(continued)

Practice Case (continued)

Date	Accounts and Explanations	PR	Debit	Credit

BUSINESS DECISION AND COMMUNICATION PROBLEM

Extended Credit Terms

Name _____

Section _____

ETHICAL DILEMMA

Interest Calculation Procedure

_____
_____
_____
_____
_____
_____
_____
_____
_____
_____
_____
_____
_____
_____
_____
_____
_____
_____
_____
_____
_____
_____
_____
_____
_____
_____
_____
_____
_____
_____
_____
_____
_____
_____
_____
_____
_____
_____
_____
_____
_____
_____
_____
_____
_____

CHAPTER 11
Inventories and Cost of Goods Sold

EXERCISES
E11-13 Computation of Inventory Cost

_____
_____
_____
_____
_____
_____
_____
_____
_____
_____
_____

E11-14 Journal Entries for Periodic and Perpetual Inventory Systems

GENERAL JOURNAL

Date	Accounts and Explanations	PR	Debit	Credit

E11-14 (continued)

GENERAL JOURNAL

Date	Accounts and Explanations	PR	Debit	Credit

E11-15 Income Statement Using Specific Identification

Income Statement

E11-16 Income Determination Using Specific Identification

Income Statement

E11-17 Inventory Valuation and Cost of Goods Sold Assuming FIFO and LIFO

E11-17 (continued)

a.

E11-17 (continued)

b.

_____

_____

_____

_____

_____

_____

_____

_____

_____

_____

_____

_____

_____

_____

_____

_____

_____

_____

_____

_____

_____

_____

_____

_____

_____

_____

_____

_____

_____

E11-18 Recordkeeping on Perpetual Records using FIFO and LIFO

FIFO Assumption

Date	Purchased			Sold			Balance		
	Qty.	Unit Cost	Total Cost	Qty.	Unit Cost	Total Cost	Qty.	Unit Cost	Total Cost

E11-18 (continued)

LIFO Assumption

Date	Purchased			Sold			Balance		
	Qty.	Unit Cost	Total Cost	Qty.	Unit Cost	Total Cost	Qty.	Unit Cost	Total Cost

E11-19 Inventory Valuation and Cost of Goods Sold Assuming Weighted Average

E11-20 Recordkeeping with Perpetual Inventory Using Moving Average

	Purchased			Sold			Balance		
Date	Qty.	Unit Cost	Total Cost	Qty.	Unit Cost	Total Cost	Qty.	Unit Cost	Total Cost

E11-21 Effect of Inventory Cost Flow Assumptions on Income Statement

a. FIFO

Income Statement

Income Statement

E11-21 (continued)

b. LIFO

Income Statement

Income Statement

E11-21 (continued)

E11-22 Three LCM Valuations and Their Effect on Gross Margin

E11-23 Estimation of Inventory by Gross Margin Method

E11-24 Estimation of Inventory by the Retail Method

E11-25 Inventory Errors

	1993	1994
Purchases		
Cost of Sales		
Gross Margin		
Inventory (end-of-year balance sheet)		
Owner's Equity (end-of-year)		

A AND B PROBLEMS

P11-26A or P11-26B Journal Entries for a Perpetual Inventory System

Requirement 1

GENERAL JOURNAL

Date	Accounts and Explanations	PR	Debit	Credit

Name _____

Section _____

P11-26A or P11-26B (continued)

Requirement 2

GENERAL JOURNAL

Date	Accounts and Explanations	PR	Debit	Credit

P11-27A or P11-27B Computation of Inventory and Cost of Goods Sold:
                     Periodic Inventory System

Requirement 1

_____

_____

_____

_____

_____

_____

_____

_____

_____

_____

_____

_____

_____

_____

_____

_____

_____

_____

_____

_____

_____

_____

_____

_____

_____

_____

_____

_____

_____

_____

_____

_____

_____

P11-27A or P11-27B (continued)

Requirement 2

_____
_____
_____
_____
_____
_____
_____
_____
_____
_____
_____
_____
_____
_____
_____
_____
_____
_____
_____
_____
_____
_____
_____
_____
_____
_____
_____
_____
_____
_____
_____

P11-27A or P11-27B (continued)

Requirement 3

_____
_____
_____
_____
_____
_____
_____
_____
_____
_____
_____
_____
_____
_____
_____
_____
_____
_____
_____
_____
_____
_____
_____
_____
_____
_____
_____
_____
_____
_____
_____
_____
_____

P11-28A or P11-28B Recordkeeping with Perpetual Inventory

Requirement 1

_____

Date		Purchased			Sold			Balance		
	Qty.	Unit Cost	Total Cost	Qty.	Unit Cost	Total Cost	Qty.	Unit Cost	Total Cost

_____
_____
_____
_____
_____
_____
_____
_____

P11-28A or P11-28B (continued)

Requirement 2

Date		Purchased			Sold			Balance		
	Qty.	Unit Cost	Total Cost	Qty.	Unit Cost	Total Cost	Qty.	Unit Cost	Total Cost

_____

_____

_____

_____

_____

P11-28A or P11-28B (continued)

Requirement 3

_____

Date	Purchased			Sold			Balance		
	Qty.	Unit Cost	Total Cost	Qty.	Unit Cost	Total Cost	Qty.	Unit Cost	Total Cost

_____
_____
_____
_____
_____

P11-29A Effect of Cost Flow Assumptions on Financial Statements in a Period of Rising Prices or

P11-29B Effect of Cost Flow Assumptions on Financial Statements in a Period of Falling Prices

_____
_____
_____
_____
_____
_____
_____
_____
_____
_____
_____
_____
_____
_____
_____
_____
_____
_____
_____
_____
_____
_____
_____
_____
_____
_____
_____
_____
_____
_____
_____
_____
_____
_____
_____
_____
_____
_____
_____

P11-29A and P11-29B (continued)

Requirement 1a

_____
_____
_____
_____
_____
_____
_____
_____
_____
_____
_____
_____
_____
_____
_____
_____
_____
_____
_____
_____
_____

Requirement 1b

_____
_____
_____
_____
_____
_____
_____
_____
_____
_____
_____
_____
_____
_____
_____
_____
_____
_____
_____
_____

P11-29A or P11-29B (continued)

Requirement 2

Comparative Income Statements

Comparative Balance Sheets

Requirement 3

_____
_____
_____
_____
_____
_____
_____
_____
_____
_____
_____

P11-29A or P11-29B (continued)

Requirement 4

_____

_____

_____

_____

_____

_____

_____

_____

_____

_____

_____

_____

_____

_____

_____

Requirement 5

_____

_____

_____

_____

_____

_____

_____

_____

_____

_____

_____

_____

_____

_____

_____

P11-29A (continued)

Requirement 6

_____
_____
_____
_____
_____
_____
_____
_____
_____
_____
_____
_____
_____
_____
_____
_____
_____

P11-30A or P11-30B Estimation of Inventories by the Gross Margin and Retail Inventory Methods

Requirement 1

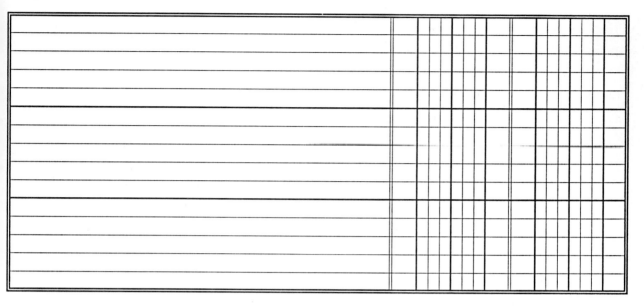

Requirement 2

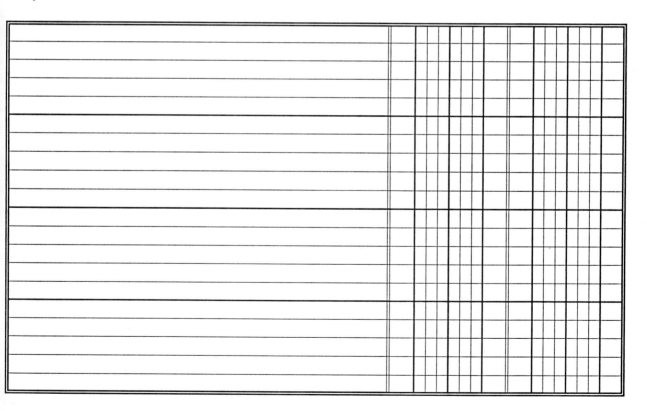

P11-31A Effect of Overstatement of Ending Inventory and Failure to Record Purchases

Requirement 1

Income Statement

Income Statement

Name _____

Section _____

P11-31A (continued)

Requirement 2

_____
_____
_____
_____
_____
_____
_____
_____
_____
_____
_____
_____
_____
_____
_____
_____
_____
_____
_____
_____
_____
_____
_____
_____
_____
_____
_____
_____

P11-31B Effect of Inventory Errors

Requirement 1

_____
_____
_____
_____
_____
_____
_____
_____
_____
_____
_____

Requirement 2

_____
_____
_____
_____
_____
_____
_____
_____
_____
_____
_____
_____
_____
_____
_____
_____
_____
_____
_____
_____
_____
_____

P11-31B (continued)

Requirement 3

_____

_____

_____

_____

_____

_____

_____

_____

_____

_____

_____

_____

_____

_____

_____

_____

_____

P11-32A Interpretation of Inventory Note to Financial Statements for Woolworth Company

P11-32B Interpretation of Inventory Note to Financial Statements for Wrigley Company

Requirement 1

_____
_____
_____
_____
_____
_____

Requirement 2

_____
_____
_____
_____
_____
_____
_____
_____
_____
_____
_____

Requirement 3

_____
_____
_____
_____
_____
_____
_____
_____
_____
_____

Requirement 4

_____
_____
_____
_____
_____
_____
_____
_____
_____
_____

Name _____

Section _____

PRACTICE CASE

Inventories and Cost of Goods Sold

Requirement 1a

Income Statement

Practice Case (continued)

Requirement 1b

Income Statement

Name _____

Section _____

Practice Case (continued)

Requirement 2a

Income Statement

Requirement 2b

Income Statement

11-43

Practice Case (continued)

Requirement 3

_____

_____

_____

_____

_____

_____

_____

_____

_____

_____

_____

_____

_____

_____

_____

_____

_____

_____

_____

_____

_____

_____

_____

_____

_____

Practice Case (continued)

Requirement 4

_____

_____

_____

_____

_____

_____

_____

_____

_____

_____

_____

_____

_____

_____

_____

_____

_____

_____

_____

_____

_____

_____

Name _____

Section _____

BUSINESS DECISION AND COMMUNICATION PROBLEM

Comparison of Inventory Cost Flow Methods for Pennzoil Company with Competing Oil Companies

_____
_____
_____
_____
_____
_____
_____
_____
_____
_____
_____
_____
_____
_____
_____
_____
_____
_____
_____
_____
_____
_____
_____
_____
_____
_____
_____
_____
_____
_____
_____
_____
_____
_____
_____
_____
_____
_____
_____
_____
_____
_____

(continued)

Business Decision and Communication Problem (continued)

Name _____

Section _____

ETHICAL DILEMMA

Managing Reported Net Income under LIFO

_____
_____
_____
_____
_____
_____
_____
_____
_____
_____
_____
_____
_____
_____
_____
_____
_____
_____
_____
_____
_____
_____
_____
_____
_____
_____
_____
_____
_____
_____
_____
_____
_____
_____
_____
_____
_____
_____
_____
_____
_____
_____
_____
_____

CHAPTER 12
Long-term Assets

EXERCISES

E12-16 Amount of Debit to Asset Account

_____
_____
_____
_____
_____
_____
_____
_____
_____
_____
_____
_____

E12-17 Recordkeeping: An Acquisition

GENERAL JOURNAL

Date	Accounts and Explanations	PR	Debit	Credit

E12-18 Recording the Cost of a New Plant

GENERAL JOURNAL

Date	Accounts and Explanations	PR	Debit	Credit

E12-19 Depreciation: All Methods (Full Year)

a.

GENERAL JOURNAL

Date	Accounts and Explanations	PR	Debit	Credit

E12-19 (continued)

b.

GENERAL JOURNAL

Date	Accounts and Explanations	PR	Debit	Credit

c.

GENERAL JOURNAL

Date	Accounts and Explanations	PR	Debit	Credit

d.

GENERAL JOURNAL

Date	Accounts and Explanations	PR	Debit	Credit

E12-20 Partial-year Depreciation: Three Methods (Partial Year Plus Full Year)

E12-21 Computation of Depreciation Expense for Financial Reporting and Cost Recovery Deduction under MACRS

_____
_____
_____
_____
_____
_____
_____
_____
_____
_____
_____
_____
_____
_____
_____
_____
_____
_____

E12-22 Computation of Depreciation Expense for Financial Reporting and Cost Recovery Deduction under MACRS

_____
_____
_____
_____
_____
_____
_____
_____
_____
_____
_____
_____
_____
_____
_____
_____
_____
_____
_____
_____
_____
_____
_____
_____
_____
_____
_____
_____
_____
_____

E12-23 Revenue and Capital Expenditures

a. _____   h. _____
b. _____   i. _____
c. _____   j. _____
d. _____   k. _____
e. _____   l. _____
f. _____   m. _____
g. _____

E12-24 Revision of Depreciation Expense

_____

_____

_____

_____

_____

_____

_____

_____

_____

_____

_____

_____

_____

_____

_____

_____

_____

_____

_____

_____

_____

_____

_____

_____

_____

Name _____

Section _____

E12-25 Overhaul and New Depreciation Amount

GENERAL JOURNAL

Date	Accounts and Explanations	PR	Debit	Credit

E12-26 Sale of a Used Asset

GENERAL JOURNAL

Date	Accounts and Explanations	PR	Debit	Credit

E12-27 Trade-in on a Similar and a Dissimilar Item

1.

GENERAL JOURNAL

Date	Accounts and Explanations	PR	Debit	Credit

2a.

GENERAL JOURNAL

Date	Accounts and Explanations	PR	Debit	Credit

E12-27 (continued)

2b.

GENERAL JOURNAL

Date	Accounts and Explanations	PR	Debit	Credit

3a.

GENERAL JOURNAL

Date	Accounts and Explanations	PR	Debit	Credit

E12-27 (continued)

3b.

GENERAL JOURNAL

Date	Accounts and Explanations	PR	Debit	Credit

E12-28 Computation of Depletion Cost

_____

_____

_____

_____

_____

_____

_____

_____

_____

_____

E12-29 Cost Allocation of Long-term Assets

a. _____   h. _____

b. _____   i. _____

c. _____   j. _____

d. _____   k. _____

e. _____   l. _____

f. _____   m. _____

g. _____

E12-30 Amortization of Franchise

GENERAL JOURNAL

Date	Accounts and Explanations	PR	Debit	Credit

E12-31 Amortization of Patent

GENERAL JOURNAL

Date	Accounts and Explanations	PR	Debit	Credit

A AND B PROBLEMS

P12-32A or P12-32B Determining the Cost of Tangible Plant Assets

Requirement 1

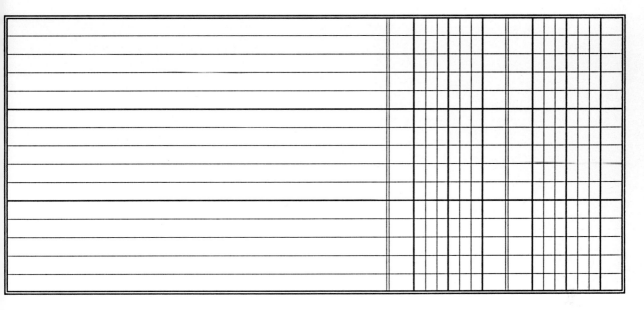

Requirement 2

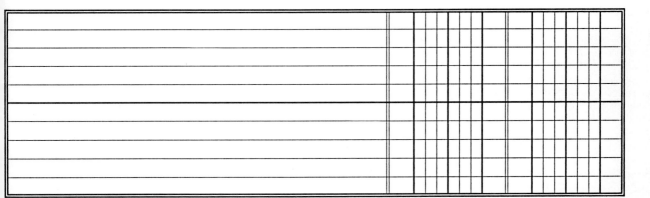

Name _____

Section _____

P12-33A or P12-33B Depreciation for Several Years: Three Methods

Requirement 1

_____
_____
_____
_____
_____
_____
_____
_____
_____
_____
_____
_____
_____
_____
_____
_____
_____

P12-33A or P12-33B (continued)

Requirement 2

GENERAL JOURNAL

Date	Accounts and Explanations	PR	Debit	Credit

P12-34A or P12-34B Overhaul and Revised Depreciation Amount

Requirement 1

GENERAL JOURNAL

Date	Accounts and Explanations	PR	Debit	Credit

Requirement 2

GENERAL JOURNAL

Date	Accounts and Explanations	PR	Debit	Credit

P12-34A or P12-34B (continued)

Requirement 3

GENERAL JOURNAL

Date	Accounts and Explanations	PR	Debit	Credit

P12-34A or P12-34B (continued)

Requirement 4

GENERAL JOURNAL

Date	Accounts and Explanations	PR	Debit	Credit

P12-35A Entries over the Life of a Plant Asset: SYD Depreciation or
P12-35B Entries over the Life of a Plant Item—Straight Line Depreciation

GENERAL JOURNAL

Date	Accounts and Explanations	PR	Debit	Credit

(continued)

P12-35A or P12-35B (continued)

Date	Accounts and Explanations	PR	Debit	Credit

P12-36A or P12-36B Exchange for Similar and Dissimilar Items

Requirement 1

GENERAL JOURNAL

Date	Accounts and Explanations	PR	Debit	Credit

Requirement 2

GENERAL JOURNAL

Date	Accounts and Explanations	PR	Debit	Credit

Name _____

Section _____

P12-36A or P12-36B (continued)

Requirement 3

GENERAL JOURNAL

Date	Accounts and Explanations	PR	Debit	Credit

Name _____

Section _____

P12-37A or P12-37B Depletion and Inventoriable Costs

Requirement 1

Requirement 2

12-27

P12-37A or P12-37B (continued)

Requirement 3

Requirement 4

Name _____

Section _____

P12-38A or P12-38B Revenue Expenditure or Capital Expenditure for Long-term Assets

12-29

Name _____

Section _____

PRACTICE CASE

Long-term Assets

GENERAL JOURNAL

Date	Accounts and Explanations	PR	Debit	Credit

(continued)

12-31

Copyright © 1992 by Harcourt Brace Jovanovich, Inc. All rights reserved.

Practice Case (continued)

Date	Accounts and Explanations	PR	Debit	Credit

(continued)

Practice Case (continued)

Date	Accounts and Explanations	PR	Debit	Credit

12-33

Name _____

Section _____

Practice Case (continued)

Name _____

Section _____

BUSINESS DECISION AND COMMUNICATION PROBLEM

Interpretation of Depreciation Note for Caterpillar, Inc.

_____

_____

_____

_____

_____

_____

_____

_____

_____

_____

_____

_____

_____

_____

_____

_____

_____

_____

_____

_____

_____

_____

_____

_____

_____

_____

_____

_____

_____

_____

_____

_____

_____

_____

_____

_____

_____

_____

_____

_____

_____

_____

(continued)

Business Decision and Communication Problem (continued)

ETHICAL DILEMMA

Depreciation Policies

MINI PRACTICE SET II
[For Requirement 1, see foldout section at back of book.]

Requirement 2

Income Statement

(continued)

Mini Practice Set Requirement 2 (continued)

Mini Practice Set Requirement 2 (continued)

Statement of Owner's Equity

Mini Practice Set Requirement 2 (continued)

Balance Sheet

(continued)

Mini Practice Set Requirement 2 (continued)

12-43

Mini Practice Set (continued)

Requirement 3

GENERAL JOURNAL

Date	Accounts and Explanations	PR	Debit	Credit

Name _____

Section _____

Mini Practice Set Requirement 3 (continued)

_____
_____
_____
_____
_____
_____
_____
_____
_____
_____
_____
_____
_____
_____
_____
_____
_____
_____

Mini Practice Set Requirement 3 (continued)

GENERAL JOURNAL

Date	Accounts and Explanations	PR	Debit	Credit

(continued)

Mini Practice Set Requirement 3 (continued)

Date		Accounts and Explanations	PR	Debit	Credit

Mini Practice Set (continued)

Requirement 4

GENERAL JOURNAL

Date	Accounts and Explanations	PR	Debit	Credit

(continued)

Mini Practice Set Requirement 4 (continued)

Date		Accounts and Explanations	PR	Debit	Credit

12-49

Mini Practice Set (continued)

Requirement 5

(continued)

Name _____

Section _____

Mini Practice Set Requirement 5 (continued)

CHAPTER 13
Financial Reporting Issues

EXERCISES

E13-21 Accounting Standards

E13-22 Installment Basis

E13-23 Percentage of Completion Method of Revenue Recognition

_____
_____
_____
_____
_____
_____
_____
_____
_____
_____
_____
_____
_____
_____
_____
_____
_____
_____
_____
_____
_____
_____
_____

E13-24 Adjustment of Sales

_____
_____
_____
_____
_____
_____
_____
_____
_____
_____
_____
_____
_____
_____
_____
_____
_____
_____
_____
_____

E13-25 Real Growth in Sales

_____
_____
_____
_____
_____
_____
_____
_____
_____
_____
_____
_____
_____
_____
_____
_____
_____
_____
_____
_____
_____
_____
_____
_____
_____
_____
_____
_____
_____
_____
_____
_____
_____
_____
_____
_____
_____
_____
_____
_____
_____
_____
_____
_____

E13-26 Adjustment of Income for Current Cost

_____
_____
_____
_____
_____
_____
_____
_____
_____
_____
_____
_____
_____
_____
_____
_____
_____
_____
_____
_____
_____
_____

E13-27 Monetary vs. Nonmonetary Assets

_____
_____
_____
_____
_____
_____
_____
_____
_____
_____
_____
_____
_____
_____
_____
_____
_____
_____
_____
_____
_____
_____
_____
_____
_____
_____
_____
_____

E13-28 Asset Adjustment with Index

1.

_____
_____
_____
_____
_____
_____
_____
_____
_____
_____

2.

_____
_____
_____
_____
_____
_____
_____
_____
_____
_____
_____
_____
_____
_____
_____

E13-29 General Price-level Adjustments: Assets

_____
_____
_____
_____
_____
_____
_____
_____
_____
_____
_____
_____
_____
_____
_____
_____

A AND B PROBLEMS

P13-30A or P13-30B Identifying GAAP

_____

(continued)

P13-30A or P13-30B (continued)

Name _____

Section _____

P13-31A or P13-31B Identifying Violations of GAAP

P13-32A or P13-32B Evaluating Financial Statements to Conform to GAAP

Income Statement

Statement of Owner's Equity

P13-32A or P13-32B (continued)

_____

Balance Sheet

_____

P13-32A or P13-32B (continued)

P13-33A Evaluating Selected Supplemental Price-level Disclosures for Digital Equipment Corporation or

P13-33B Evaluating Selected Supplemental Price-level Disclosures for Gulf & Western Industries, Inc.

P13-33A or P13-33B (continued)

Requirement 2

_____

_____

_____

_____

_____

_____

_____

_____

_____

_____

_____

_____

_____

_____

_____

_____

_____

_____

_____

_____

_____

_____

_____

P13-34A Interpreting Supplemental Inflation-related Information for UST Corporation

Requirement 1

_____
_____
_____
_____
_____
_____
_____
_____
_____
_____
_____

Requirement 2

_____
_____
_____
_____
_____
_____
_____
_____
_____
_____
_____

P13-34A (continued)

Requirement 3

_____
_____
_____
_____
_____
_____
_____
_____
_____
_____
_____
_____
_____
_____
_____
_____
_____
_____
_____
_____
_____
_____
_____
_____
_____

P13-34B Comparing Historical Cost, Constant Dollar, and Current Cost Information

Requirement 1

_____
_____
_____
_____
_____
_____
_____
_____
_____
_____
_____
_____
_____
_____
_____
_____
_____
_____
_____
_____
_____
_____
_____
_____

Requirement 2

_____
_____
_____
_____
_____

P13-35A (Appendix 13A) Computing a Purchasing Power Gain on Net Monetary Items or

P13-35B (Appendix 13A) Computing a Purchasing Power Loss on Net Monetary Items

---

(continued)

Name _____

Section _____

P13-35A or P13-35B (continued)

_____
_____
_____
_____
_____
_____
_____
_____
_____
_____
_____
_____
_____
_____
_____
_____
_____
_____
_____
_____
_____
_____
_____
_____
_____
_____
_____
_____
_____
_____
_____
_____
_____
_____
_____
_____
_____

P13-36A (Appendix 13A) Preparing Price-level Disclosures during a Period of Inflation or

P13-36B (Appendix 13A) Preparing Price-level Disclosures during a Period of Deflation

Requirement 1

_____

Income Statement Adjusted for Changing Prices

_____

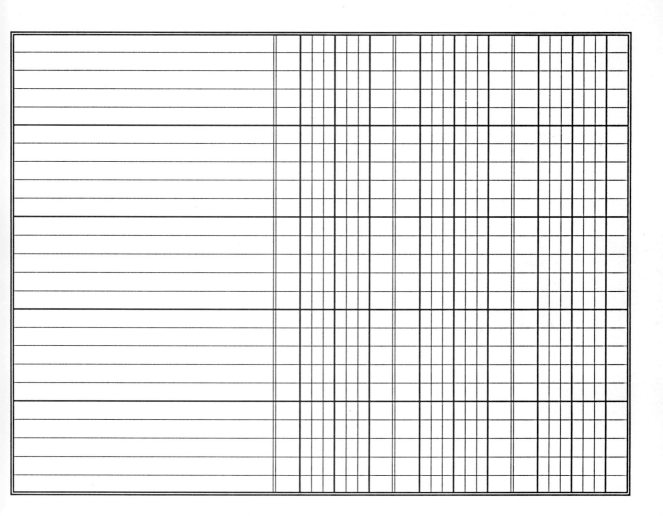

P13-36A or P13-36B Requirement 1 (continued)

(continued)

Name _____

Section _____

P13-36A or P13-36B Requirement 1 (continued)

(continued)

P13-36A or P13-36B Requirement 1 (continued)

P13-36A or P13-36B (continued)

Requirement 2

_____

PRACTICE CASE

Preparing Corrected Financial Statements

Requirement 1

Income Statement

Statement of Owner's Equity

Name _____

Section _____

Practice Case Requirement 1 (continued)

Balance Sheet

Name _____

Section _____

Practice Case (continued)

Requirement 2

_____
_____
_____
_____
_____
_____
_____
_____
_____
_____
_____
_____
_____
_____
_____
_____

Practice Case (continued)

Requirement 3

_____
_____
_____
_____
_____
_____
_____
_____
_____
_____
_____
_____
_____
_____
_____
_____
_____
_____
_____
_____
_____
_____
_____
_____
_____
_____
_____
_____
_____
_____
_____
_____
_____
_____
_____
_____
_____
_____
_____
_____
_____
_____
_____
_____
_____
_____
_____

(continued)

Name _____

Section _____

Practice Case Requirement 3 (continued)

BUSINESS DECISION AND COMMUNICATION PROBLEM

Is a Withdrawal in Order?

_____
_____
_____
_____
_____
_____
_____
_____
_____
_____
_____
_____
_____
_____
_____
_____
_____
_____
_____
_____
_____
_____
_____
_____
_____
_____
_____
_____
_____
_____
_____
_____
_____
_____
_____
_____
_____
_____
_____
_____
_____
_____
_____
_____

(continued)

Name _____

Section _____

Business Decision and Communication Problem (continued)

ETHICAL DILEMMA

Failure to Disclose Loss of a Major Customer and Sale of Stock by Management

_____
_____
_____
_____
_____
_____
_____
_____
_____
_____
_____
_____
_____
_____
_____
_____
_____
_____
_____
_____
_____
_____
_____
_____
_____
_____
_____
_____
_____
_____
_____
_____
_____
_____
_____
_____
_____
_____
_____
_____
_____
_____
_____
_____
_____

Name _____

Section _____

EXERCISES

E14-13 Recording Investment of Cash and Noncash Assets by Partners

GENERAL JOURNAL

Date	Accounts and Explanations	PR	Debit	Credit

E14-14 Recording Transactions by Partners

GENERAL JOURNAL

Date	Accounts and Explanations	PR	Debit	Credit

E14-15 Dividing Income with Interest Allowance

_____

_____

_____

_____

_____

_____

_____

_____

_____

_____

_____

_____

_____

_____

_____

_____

E14-16 Dividing Income with Salary Allowance

_____

_____

_____

_____

_____

_____

_____

_____

_____

_____

_____

_____

_____

_____

_____

E14-17 Dividing Income with Interest and Salary Allowance

_____
_____
_____
_____
_____
_____
_____
_____
_____
_____
_____
_____
_____
_____
_____
_____
_____
_____
_____
_____
_____

E14-18 Preparing Financial Statements

1.

Income Statement

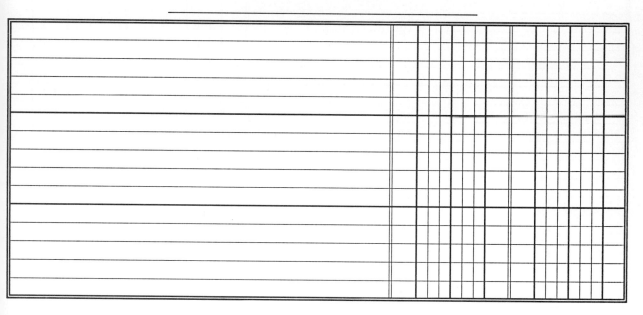

Statement of Partners' Equity

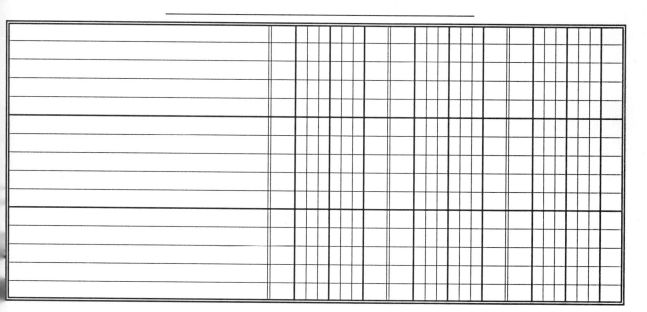

E14-18 (continued)

Balance Sheet

E14-18 (continued)

2.

_____
_____
_____
_____
_____
_____
_____
_____
_____
_____
_____
_____

E14-19 Admitting a New Partner by Purchase of Interest from an Existing Partner

GENERAL JOURNAL

Date	Accounts and Explanations	PR	Debit	Credit

E14-20 Admitting a New Partner

1.

GENERAL JOURNAL

Date	Accounts and Explanations	PR	Debit	Credit

2.

GENERAL JOURNAL

Date	Accounts and Explanations	PR	Debit	Credit

E14-20 (continued)

3.

GENERAL JOURNAL

Date	Accounts and Explanations	PR	Debit	Credit

E14-21 Recording Withdrawal of a Partner

GENERAL JOURNAL

Date	Accounts and Explanations	PR	Debit	Credit

Name _____

Section _____

E14-22 Recording Withdrawal by Death of a Partner

GENERAL JOURNAL

Date	Accounts and Explanations	PR	Debit	Credit

E14-23 Liquidating a Partnership

Statement of Liquidation

	Cash	Other Assets		Capital	
			Anders	Baker	Card

14-12

E14-24 Liquidating a Partnership with Deficiency

Statement of Liquidation

Cash	Other Assets	Capital		
		Dawson	Eason	Foster

Name _____

Section _____

E14-24 (continued)

A AND B PROBLEMS

P14-25A or P14-25B Recording Investments of Partners under Different Situations

Requirement 1

GENERAL JOURNAL

Date	Accounts and Explanations	PR	Debit	Credit

Requirement 2

Date	Accounts and Explanations	PR	Debit	Credit

14-15

P14-25A or P14-25B (continued)

Requirement 3

Date		Accounts and Explanations	PR	Debit	Credit

Requirement 4

Date		Accounts and Explanations	PR	Debit	Credit

P14-26A or P14-26B Dividing Income under Various Assumptions

Requirement 1

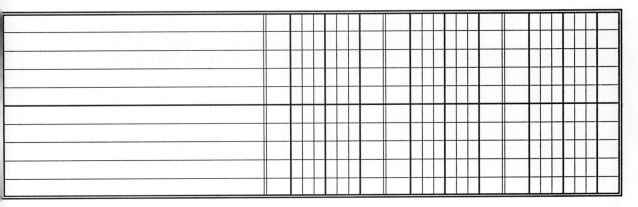

Requirement 2

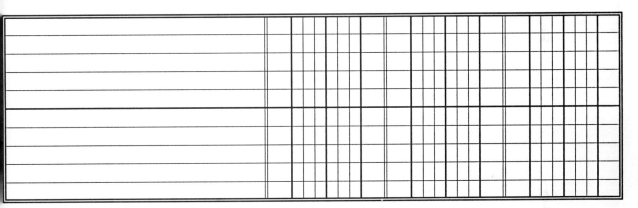

Requirement 3

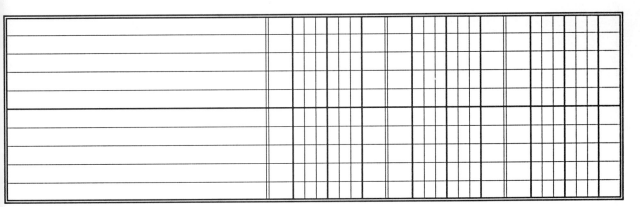

P14-26A or P14-26B (continued)

Requirement 4

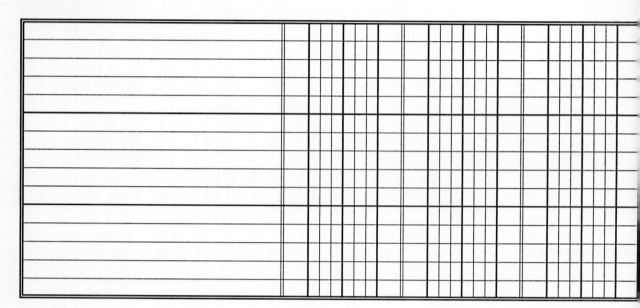

P14-27A or P14-27B Distributing Profits and Losses

Requirement 1

GENERAL JOURNAL

Date	Accounts and Explanations	PR	Debit	Credit

Requirement 2

Date	Accounts and Explanations	PR	Debit	Credit

P14-27A or P14-27B (continued)

Requirement 3

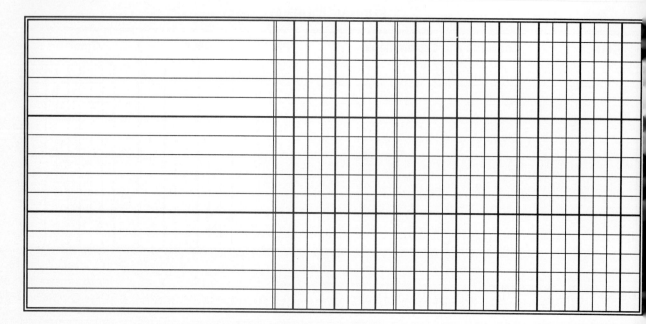

GENERAL JOURNAL

Date		Accounts and Explanations	PR	Debit	Credit

P14-28A or P14-28B Preparing Financial Statements for a Partnership

Requirement 1

Income Statement

Requirement 2

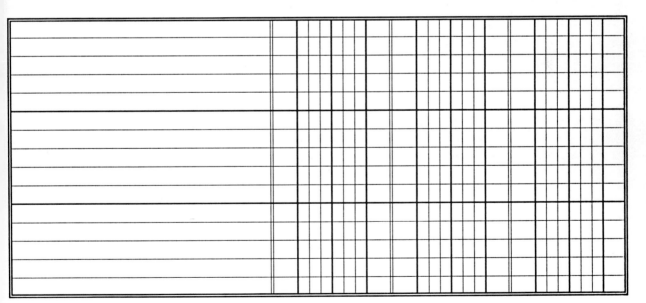

P14-28A or P14-28B (continued)

Requirement 3

Statement of Partners' Equity

Name ____________________

Section ____________________

P14-28A or P14-28B (continued)

Requirement 4

____

Balance Sheet

____

P14-29A or P14-29B Admitting a New Partner under Various Assumptions

Requirement 1

GENERAL JOURNAL

Date	Accounts and Explanations	PR	Debit	Credit

Requirement 2

_____

_____

_____

_____

_____

GENERAL JOURNAL

Date	Accounts and Explanations	PR	Debit	Credit

P14-29A or P14-29B (continued)

Requirement 3

_____
_____
_____
_____
_____

GENERAL JOURNAL

Date	Accounts and Explanations	PR	Debit	Credit

Requirement 4

_____
_____
_____
_____
_____

GENERAL JOURNAL

Date	Accounts and Explanations	PR	Debit	Credit

P14-29A or P14-29B (continued)

Requirement 5

_____
_____
_____
_____
_____

GENERAL JOURNAL

Date	Accounts and Explanations	PR	Debit	Credit

Requirement 6

_____
_____
_____
_____
_____

GENERAL JOURNAL

Date	Accounts and Explanations	PR	Debit	Credit

P14-30A or P14-30B Recording the Withdrawal of a Partner under Different Conditions

Requirement 1

GENERAL JOURNAL

Date	Accounts and Explanations	PR	Debit	Credit

Requirement 2

_____

_____

_____

_____

_____

GENERAL JOURNAL

Date	Accounts and Explanations	PR	Debit	Credit

P14-30A or P14-30B (continued)

Requirement 3

_____
_____
_____
_____
_____

GENERAL JOURNAL

Date	Accounts and Explanations	PR	Debit	Credit

P14-31A or P14-31B Preparing a Statement of Liquidation

Statement of Liquidation

Cash	Other Assets	Liabilities	Capital		
			Sawyer	Finn	Twain

P14-31A or P14-31B (continued)

PRACTICE CASE

Partnerships

GENERAL JOURNAL

Page _____

Date	Accounts and Explanations	PR	Debit	Credit

(continued)

Practice Case (continued)

Date	Accounts and Explanations	PR	Debit	Credit

(continued)

14-34

Practice Case (continued)

Date	Accounts and Explanations	PR	Debit	Credit

14-35

Practice Case (continued)

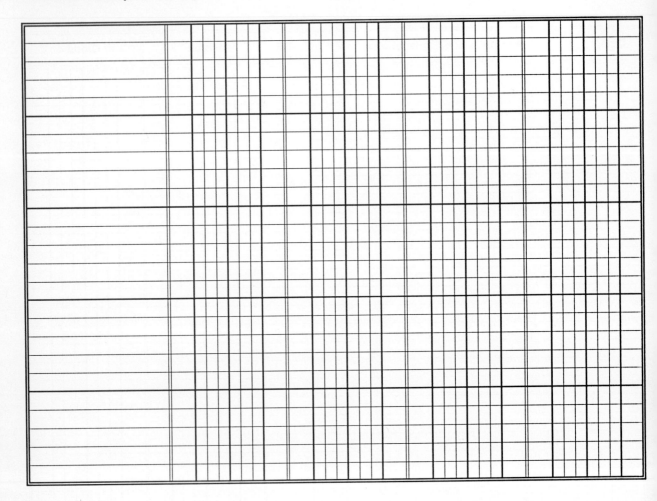

Practice Case (continued)

Statement of Liquidation

	Cash	Other Assets	Liabilities	Capital		
				J. Cash	P. Wagner	J. Wayne

14-37

Practice Case (continued)

BUSINESS DECISION AND COMMUNICATION PROBLEM

Forming a Partnership

(continued)

Business Decision and Communication Problem (continued)

ETHICAL DILEMMA

Abuse of Partnership Relationship

14-41

CHAPTER 15
Corporations: Paid-In Capital

EXERCISES
E15-15 Identifying Sources of Stockholders' Equity

1.

_____
_____
_____
_____
_____
_____
_____
_____
_____
_____
_____
_____
_____
_____
_____
_____
_____
_____
_____
_____
_____
_____
_____
_____
_____
_____

E15-15 (continued)

2.

<u>Partial Balance Sheet</u>

Partial Balance Sheet

Name _____

Section _____

E15-16 Identifying Key Terms Used to Define and Measure Elements in Paid-in Capital

_____
_____
_____
_____
_____
_____
_____
_____
_____
_____
_____
_____
_____
_____
_____
_____

E15-17 Identifying Key Terms Used to Define and Measure Elements of Paid-in Capital

_____
_____
_____
_____
_____
_____
_____
_____
_____
_____
_____
_____
_____
_____
_____
_____
_____
_____
_____
_____
_____
_____

E15-18 Recording Common Stock Transactions

GENERAL JOURNAL

Date	Accounts and Explanations	PR	Debit	Credit

E15-19 Recording Par Value Common Stock

GENERAL JOURNAL

Date	Accounts and Explanations	PR	Debit	Credit

E15-20 Issuing Common Stock for Cash and Noncash Items

GENERAL JOURNAL

Date	Accounts and Explanations	PR	Debit	Credit

(continued)

E15-20 (continued)

Date	Accounts and Explanations	PR	Debit	Credit

E15-21 Recording Common Stock Subscriptions

GENERAL JOURNAL

Date	Accounts and Explanations	PR	Debit	Credit

(continued)

E15-21 (continued)

Date		Accounts and Explanations	PR	Debit	Credit

E15-22 Calculating the Cash Collections from Stock Transactions

E15-23 Recording Donated Assets

GENERAL JOURNAL

Date	Accounts and Explanations	PR	Debit	Credit

E15-24 Recording Common Stock Transactions and Donation of Assets

GENERAL JOURNAL

Date	Accounts and Explanations	PR	Debit	Credit

E15-25 Preparing Paid-in Capital Section of Balance Sheet

Partial Balance Sheet

E15-26 Recording Various Common and Preferred Stock Issues

GENERAL JOURNAL

Date	Accounts and Explanations	PR	Debit	Credit

(continued)

Name _____

Section _____

E15-26 (continued)

Date		Accounts and Explanations	PR	Debit	Credit

A AND B PROBLEMS

P15-27A or P15-27B Identifying Key Terms and Computing Elements of Paid-in Capital

Requirement 1

_____
_____
_____
_____
_____
_____
_____
_____
_____
_____
_____
_____
_____
_____
_____
_____
_____
_____
_____
_____
_____
_____
_____
_____
_____
_____
_____
_____

Requirement 2

_____
_____
_____
_____
_____
_____
_____
_____
_____
_____
_____
_____
_____
_____

P15-28A Recording Stockholders' Common Stock Transactions and Calculating Account Balances

Requirement 1

GENERAL JOURNAL

Date	Accounts and Explanations	PR	Debit	Credit

(continued)

P15-28A Requirement 1 (continued)

Date	Accounts and Explanations	PR	Debit	Credit

P15-28A (continued)

Requirement 2

P15-28B Recording Common Stock Transactions and Preparing the Paid-in Capital Portion of Balance Sheet

Requirement 1

GENERAL JOURNAL

Date	Accounts and Explanations	PR	Debit	Credit

(continued)

Name _____

Section _____

P15-28B Requirement 1 (continued)

Date	Accounts and Explanations	PR	Debit	Credit

15-22

P15-28B (continued)

Requirement 2

Partial Balance Sheet

P15-29A or P15-29B Recording Capital Stock Transactions and Preparing the Paid-in Capital Portion of a Balance Sheet

Requirement 1

GENERAL JOURNAL

Page _____

Date	Accounts and Explanations	PR	Debit	Credit

(continued)

P15-29A or P15-29B Requirement 1 (continued)

Date	Accounts and Explanations	PR	Debit	Credit

(continued)

P15-29A or P15-29B Requirement 1 (continued)

Date	Accounts and Explanations	PR	Debit	Credit

P15-29A or P15-29B (continued)

Requirement 2

GENERAL LEDGER

_____ Acct. No. _____

Date	Explanation	PR	Debit	Credit	Balance	
					Debit	Credit

_____ Acct. No. _____

Date	Explanation	PR	Debit	Credit	Balance	
					Debit	Credit

_____ Acct. No. _____

Date	Explanation	PR	Debit	Credit	Balance	
					Debit	Credit

P15-29A or P15-29B Requirement 2 (continued)

_____ Acct. No. _____

Date	Explanation	PR	Debit	Credit	Balance	
					Debit	Credit

_____ Acct. No. _____

Date	Explanation	PR	Debit	Credit	Balance	
					Debit	Credit

_____ Acct. No. _____

Date	Explanation	PR	Debit	Credit	Balance	
					Debit	Credit

P15-29A or P15-29B Requirement 2 (continued)

Acct. No. _____

Date	Explanation	PR	Debit	Credit	Balance	
					Debit	Credit

Acct. No. _____

Date	Explanation	PR	Debit	Credit	Balance	
					Debit	Credit

Acct. No. _____

Date	Explanation	PR	Debit	Credit	Balance	
					Debit	Credit

P15-29A or P15-29B (continued)

Requirement 3

Partial Balance Sheet

P15-30A or P15-30B Recording Various Stock Transactions and Preparing the Stockholders' Equity Section of a Balance Sheet

Requirements 1 and 3

GENERAL LEDGER

_____ Acct. No. _____

Date	Explanation	PR	Debit	Credit	Balance Debit	Balance Credit

_____ Acct. No. _____

Date	Explanation	PR	Debit	Credit	Balance Debit	Balance Credit

_____ Acct. No. _____

Date	Explanation	PR	Debit	Credit	Balance Debit	Balance Credit

P15-30A or P15-30B Requirements 1 and 3 (continued)

_____ Acct. No. _____

Date	Explanation	PR	Debit	Credit	Balance Debit	Balance Credit

Requirement 2

GENERAL JOURNAL
Page _____

Date	Accounts and Explainations	PR	Debit	Credit

(continued)

P15-30A or P15-30B Requirement 2 (continued)

Date	Accounts and Explanations	PR	Debit	Credit

P15-30A or P15-30B (continued)

Requirement 4

Partial Balance Sheet

P15-31A or P15-31B Reconstructing Journal Entries for Capital Stock Transactions

Requirement 1

GENERAL JOURNAL

Date	Accounts and Explanations	PR	Debit	Credit

(continued)

Name _____

Section _____

P15-31A or P15-31B Requirement 1 (continued)

Date		Accounts and Explanations	PR	Debit	Credit

Requirement 2

_____
_____
_____
_____
_____
_____
_____
_____
_____
_____
_____
_____
_____
_____
_____
_____

Name _____

Section _____

P15-32A or P15-32B Preparing the Stockholders' Equity Section of a Balance Sheet

_____

Partial Balance Sheet

_____

P15-33A or P15-33B Interpreting Stockholders' Equity Information

Requirement 1

_____
_____
_____
_____
_____

Requirement 2

_____
_____
_____
_____
_____
_____
_____
_____
_____
_____
_____
_____
_____

Requirement 3

_____
_____
_____
_____
_____

Requirement 4

_____
_____
_____
_____
_____

PRACTICE CASE

Corporations: Paid-in Capital

Requirement 1

GENERAL JOURNAL

Date	Accounts and Explanations	PR	Debit	Credit

(continued)

15-43

Practice Case Requirement 1 (continued)

Date	Accounts and Explanations	PR	Debit	Credit

(continued)

Name _____

Section _____

Practice Case Requirement 1 (continued)

Date	Accounts and Explanations	PR	Debit	Credit

15-45

Practice Case (continued)

Requirement 2

Balance Sheet

(continued)

Practice Case Requirement 2 (continued)

Requirement 3

_____
_____
_____
_____
_____
_____
_____
_____
_____
_____
_____
_____
_____
_____
_____
_____
_____
_____
_____
_____
_____
_____
_____

Requirement 4

_____
_____
_____
_____
_____

BUSINESS DECISION AND COMMUNICATION PROBLEM

The Decision to Incorporate

_____
_____
_____
_____
_____
_____
_____
_____
_____
_____
_____
_____
_____
_____
_____
_____
_____
_____
_____
_____
_____
_____
_____
_____
_____
_____
_____
_____
_____
_____
_____
_____
_____
_____
_____
_____
_____
_____
_____
_____
_____
_____
_____
_____
_____

(continued)

15-49

Business Decision and Communication Problem (continued)

Name _____

Section _____

ETHICAL DILEMMA

Valuing Assets Acquired for Stock

_____

15-51

CHAPTER 16
Additional Stockholders' Equity Transactions and Income Disclosures

EXERCISES
E16-15 Determining the Effect of Transactions on Retained Earnings

a. _____   f. _____
b. _____   g. _____
c. _____   h. _____
d. _____   i. _____
e. _____   j. _____

E16-16 Recording Cash Dividends

GENERAL JOURNAL

Date	Accounts and Explanations	PR	Debit	Credit

E16-17 Calculating Dividends

Name _____

Section _____

E16-18 Recording a Small Stock Dividend

1.

GENERAL JOURNAL

Date	Accounts and Explanations	PR	Debit	Credit

2.

_____

_____

_____

_____

_____

E16-19 Effects of Stock Dividends and Stock Splits

1.

GENERAL JOURNAL

Date	Accounts and Explanations	PR	Debit	Credit

E16-19 (continued)

2.

E16-20 Recording Treasury Stock Transactions

GENERAL JOURNAL

Date	Accounts and Explanations	PR	Debit	Credit

Name _____

Section _____

E16-21 Recording Treasury Stock Transactions

GENERAL JOURNAL

Date	Accounts and Explanations	PR	Debit	Credit

E16-22 Recording Stock and Cash Dividends with Treasury Stock

GENERAL JOURNAL

Date	Accounts and Explanations	PR	Debit	Credit

(continued)

E16-22 (continued)

Date	Accounts and Explanations	PR	Debit	Credit

E16-23 Calculating Book Value per Share

1.

2.

E16-24 Preparing a Stockholders' Equity Section

_____

Partial Balance Sheet

_____

E16-25 Income Statement Disclosures

Income Statement

E16-26 Calculating Earnings per Share for a Simple Capital Structure

E16-27 Calculating Earnings per Share for a Complex Capital Structure

(continued)

E16-27 (continued)

A AND B PROBLEMS

P16-28A or P16-28B Journalizing Various Stockholders' Equity Transactions

GENERAL JOURNAL

Date	Accounts and Explanations	PR	Debit	Credit

(continued)

P16-28A or P16-28B (continued)

Date	Accounts and Explanations	PR	Debit	Credit

P16-29A or P16-29B Journalizing Various Stockholders' Equity Transactions and Preparing a Stockholders' Equity Section

Requirement 1

GENERAL JOURNAL

Page _____

Date	Accounts and Explanations	PR	Debit	Credit

(continued)

P16-29A or P16-29B Requirement 1 (continued)

Date		Accounts and Explanations	PR	Debit	Credit

P16-29A or P16-29B (continued)

Requirement 2

GENERAL LEDGER

_____ Acct. No. _____

Date	Explanation	PR	Debit	Credit	Balance	
					Debit	**Credit**

_____ Acct. No. _____

Date	Explanation	PR	Debit	Credit	Balance	
					Debit	**Credit**

_____ Acct. No. _____

Date	Explanation	PR	Debit	Credit	Balance	
					Debit	**Credit**

_____ Acct. No. _____

Date	Explanation	PR	Debit	Credit	Balance	
					Debit	**Credit**

P16-29A or P16-29B Requirement 2 (continued)

_____ Acct. No. _____

Date	Explanation	PR	Debit	Credit	Balance	
					Debit	Credit

_____ Acct. No. _____

Date	Explanation	PR	Debit	Credit	Balance	
					Debit	Credit

_____ Acct. No. _____

Date	Explanation	PR	Debit	Credit	Balance	
					Debit	Credit

_____ Acct. No. _____

Date	Explanation	PR	Debit	Credit	Balance	
					Debit	Credit

16-22

P16-29A or P16-29B Requirement 2 (continued)

_____ Acct. No. _____

Date	Explanation	PR	Debit	Credit	Balance Debit	Balance Credit

P16-29A or P16-29B (continued)

Requirement 3

Partial Balance Sheet

P16-30A or P16-30B Journalizing Various Stockholders' Equity Transactions and Preparing a Stockholders' Equity Section

Requirement 1

GENERAL JOURNAL

Date	Accounts and Explanations	PR	Debit	Credit

(continued)

P16-30A or P16-30B Requirement 1 (continued)

Date	Accounts and Explanations	PR	Debit	Credit

(continued)

P16-30A or P16-30B Requirement 1 (continued)

Date		Accounts and Explanations	PR	Debit	Credit

P16-30A or P16-30B Requirement 1 (continued)

GENERAL LEDGER

_____ Acct. No. _____

Date	Explanation	PR	Debit	Credit	Balance	
					Debit	Credit

_____ Acct. No. _____

Date	Explanation	PR	Debit	Credit	Balance	
					Debit	Credit

_____ Acct. No. _____

Date	Explanation	PR	Debit	Credit	Balance	
					Debit	Credit

P16-30A or P16-30B Requirement 1 (continued)

_____ Acct. No. _____

Date	Explanation	PR	Debit	Credit	Balance	
					Debit	Credit

_____ Acct. No. _____

Date	Explanation	PR	Debit	Credit	Balance	
					Debit	Credit

_____ Acct. No. _____

Date	Explanation	PR	Debit	Credit	Balance	
					Debit	Credit

P16-30A or P16-30B Requirement 1 (continued)

_____ Acct. No. _____

Date	Explanation	PR	Debit	Credit	Balance	
					Debit	Credit

Requirement 2

_____

Partial Balance Sheet

_____

P16-31A or P16-31B Determining Book Value per Share

Requirement 1

Requirement 2

Requirement 3

_____

_____

_____

_____

_____

_____

_____

_____

_____

_____

_____

_____

_____

_____

_____

16-31

P16-31A or P16-31B (continued)

Requirement 4

_____
_____
_____
_____
_____
_____
_____
_____
_____
_____
_____
_____
_____
_____
_____
_____
_____
_____
_____
_____
_____
_____
_____
_____

P16-32A or P16-32B Income Statement Disclosures

Requirement 1

Income Statement

(continued)

P16-32A or P16-32B Requirement 1 (continued)

Requirement 2

Name _____

Section _____

P16-33A or P16-33B Calculating Earnings per Share for a Simple Capital Structure

16-35

P16-34A Calculating Earnings per Share for a Complex Capital Structure

Requirement 1

P16-34A (continued)

Requirement 2

P16-34B Calculating Net Loss per Share for a Complex Capital Structure

Requirement 1

Requirement 2

PRACTICE CASE

Corporations: Retained Earnings, Dividends, Treasury Stock, and Book Value

Requirement 1

GENERAL JOURNAL

Date	Accounts and Explanations	PR	Debit	Credit

(continued)

16-41

Practice Case Requirement 1 (continued)

Date		Accounts and Explanations	PR	Debit	Credit

Practice Case (continued)

Requirement 2

Partial Balance Sheet

Practice Case (continued)

Requirement 3

Requirement 4

Name _____

Section _____

BUSINESS DECISION AND COMMUNICATION PROBLEM

Purchase of Treasury Stock by CBS, Inc.

(continued)

16-45

Business Decision and Communication Problem (continued)

ETHICAL DILEMMA

Proposed Change in Accounting Methods to Increase Net Income

_____
_____
_____
_____
_____
_____
_____
_____
_____
_____
_____
_____
_____
_____
_____
_____
_____
_____
_____
_____
_____
_____
_____
_____
_____
_____
_____
_____
_____
_____
_____
_____
_____
_____
_____
_____
_____
_____
_____
_____
_____
_____
_____
_____
_____
_____

16-47